RALPH STORER is an ex... ...has hiked and backpacked e... ...ng a Sassenach by birth, he h... ...ology at Dundee University and... ...here he can be seen in all wea... ...and tramping the tops. As well as disappearing into the hills for a regular fix of nature, he also writes novels and sexological non-fiction, and produces dark-wave music on his home computer.

Baffies' Easy Munro Guide, Volume 1: Southern Highlands is the first volume in a series that draws on his decades of experience in finding easy ways up the Scottish mountains.

Praise for his complementary series *The Ultimate Guide to the Munros*

This is a truly indispensible guide for the Munro-bagger. Bursting with information, wit and a delightful irreverence rarely found in this type of guide, it's a joy to read. Ralph and his motley crew are the perfect companions on a great day out. An absolute gem! ALEX MacKINNON, Manager, Waterstone's George Street, Edinburgh

The Ultimate Guide to The Munros *picks up where others – including my own – leave off, with lots of nitty-gritty information on alternative routes, levels of difficulty and aids to navigation, all in a very up-beat style... I look forward to seeing the rest of his fun-packed Munros series.* CAMERON MCNEISH

Fabulously illustrated...Entertaining as well as informative... One of the definitive guides to the Munros. PRESS & JOURNAL

Irresistibly funny and useful; an innovatively thought-through guide-book that makes an appetising broth of its wit, experience and visual and literary tools. Brilliant. OUTDOOR WRITERS & PHOTOGRAPHERS GUILD

After much praise and cult following from avid Munro baggers following the first book comes the second volume in The Ultimate Guide to the Munros *series... Ralph Storer preserves the quirky charm that made the first book a loveable essential for hill walkers... the book is as fun as it is practical...* EDINBURGH EVENING NEWS

While most climbing authors appear to have had their funny bones surgically removed, Storer is happy to share numerous irreverent insights into the hills, and this acts as a timely reminder that walking should, after all, be primarily about enjoyment of the great outdoors. A further advantage is that the book will easily fit in a rucksack and does not require SAS training to lug it up the slopes. SCOTTISH FIELD

With the winning combination of reliable advice and quirky humour, this is the ideal hillwalking companion. SCOTS MAGAZINE

His books are exceptional... Storer subverts the guidebook genre completely... Storer's effort would be the bedtime reading, the one where I might laugh out loud, and it contains the passages to quote to the fearful Mrs Warbeck – who would of course be memorising every pronouncement by Baffies. THE ANGRY CORRIE

BY THE SAME AUTHOR:

100 Best Routes on Scottish Mountains (Little Brown)
50 Best Routes on Skye and Raasay (Birlinn)
50 Classic Routes on Scottish Mountains (Luath Press)
Exploring Scottish Hill Tracks (Little Brown)
The Joy of Hillwalking (Luath Press)
Mountain Trivia Challenge (Cordee)
Love Scenes (a novel) (Birlinn)

The Ultimate Guide to the Munros series (Luath Press):
    Volume 1: Southern Highlands
    Volume 2: Central Highlands South (including Glen Coe)
    Volume 3: Central Highlands North (including Ben Nevis)

Baffies' Easy Munro Guide

Volume 1: Southern Highlands

RALPH STORER

Boot-tested and compiled by
Baffies, Entertainments Convenor
The Go-Take-a-Hike Mountaineering Club

Luath Press Limited

EDINBURGH

www.luath.co.uk

For Judith

First published 2012

ISBN: 978-1-908373-08-3

The paper used in this book is recyclable. It is made from low-chlorine pulps produced in a low-energy, low-emission manner from renewable forests.

Printed and bound by Bell and Bain Ltd., Glasgow

Typeset in Tahoma by Ralph Storer

CONTENTS

PREFACE

So you want to climb Munros but have understandable concerns that you may end up teetering precariously above an abysmal drop, sitting gingerly astride a knife-edge ridge or groping futilely for handfuls of grass on a crumbling rock ledge. If possible, you'd like to make it down to the foot of the mountain again. In one piece. Before dusk.

Let me introduce you to your new best friend: Baffies, the Entertainments Convenor of the Go-Take-a-Hike Mountaineering Club. In his club bio he lists himself as someone who is allergic to exertion, is prone to lassitude, suffers from altitude sickness above 600m, blisters easily and bleeds readily. However meagre your hillwalking credentials, if he can make it to the summit, so can you.

Our sister publication *The Ultimate Guide to the Munros* does what it says on the cover and describes routes of *all* kinds up *all* of the Munros. Not *all* of these are suitable for sensitive souls such as Baffies, hence the decision to 'delegate' him to write the guide-book you now hold in your hands.

When the club committee first suggested to him that he was the ideal person for the task, he almost choked on his triple chocolate layer cake. Only after we had managed to hold him down long enough to explain the book's remit did he come to embrace the idea. Indeed, he set about researching the contents with such a hitherto unseen fervour and thoroughness that we are proud to have the results associated with the club's name – a guidebook dedicated to finding easy ways up Munros.

Herein you will find easy walking routes up 25 Munros (and more!) – routes that require no rock climbing, no scrambling, no tightrope walking, no technical expertise whatsoever. Of course, hillwalking can never be a risk-free activity. No Munro is as easy to reach from an armchair as the TV remote. You will be expected to be able to put one foot in front of the other... and repeat.

Given that proviso, you will find no easier way to climb Munros than to follow in the footsteps of Baffies. I leave you in his capable hands.

Ralph Storer, President
Go-Take-a-Hike Mountaineering Club

INTRODUCTION

OF MOUNTAINS AND MUNROS

It's a big place, the Scottish Highlands. It contains so many mountains that even resident hillwalkers struggle to climb them all in a lifetime. How many mountains? That depends...

If two summits 100m apart are separated by a shallow dip, do they constitute two mountains or one mountain with two tops? If the latter, then exactly how far apart do they have to be, and how deep does the intervening dip have to be, before they become two separate mountains?

Sir Hugh Munro (1856–1919), the third President of the Scottish Mountaineering Club, tackled this problem when he published his 'Tables of Heights over 3000 Feet' in the 1891 edition of the SMC Journal. Choosing the criterion of 3000ft in the imperial system of measurement as his cut-off point, he counted 283 separate Mountains and a further 255 Tops that were over 3000ft but not sufficiently separated from a Mountain to be considered separate Mountains themselves.

In a country whose vertical axis ranges from 0ft to 4409ft (1344m) at the summit of Ben Nevis, the choice of 3000ft as a cut-off point is aesthetically justifiable and gives a satisfying number of Mountains. A metric cut-off point of 1000m (3280ft), giving a more humble 137 Mountains, has never captured the hillgoing imagination.

Unfortunately Sir Hugh omitted to leave to posterity the criteria he used to distinguish Mountains from Tops, and Tops from other highpoints over 3000ft. In his notes to the Tables he even broached the impossibility of ever making definitive distinctions. Consider, for example, the problem of differentiating between Mountains, Tops and other highpoints on the

This irresistible invitation will be found near the start of one of the routes in this book.

Sir Hugh Munro himself never became a Munroist (someone who has climbed all the Munros). Of the Tables of the day, he climbed all but three: the Inaccessible Pinnacle (although that did not become a Munro until 1921), Carn an Fhidhleir and Carn Cloich-mhuilinn. The latter, which he was saving until last because it was close to his home, was ironically demoted to Top status in 1981.

Cairngorm plateaus, where every knoll surpasses 3000ft.

The Tables were a substantial achievement in an age when mapping of the Highlands was still rudimentary, but no sooner did they appear than their definitiveness become the subject of debate. In subsequent years Munro continued to fine-tune them, using new sources such as the Revised Six-inch Survey of the late 1890s. His notes formed the basis of a new edition of the Tables, published posthumously in 1921, which listed 276 separate Mountains (now known as Munros) and 267 Tops.

The 1921 edition also included J. Rooke Corbett's list of mountains with heights between 2500ft and 3000ft ('Corbetts'), and Percy Donald's list of hills in the Scottish Lowlands of 2000ft or over ('Donalds'). Corbett's test for a separate mountain was that it needed a re-ascent of 500ft (c150m) on all sides. Donald's test was more mathematical. A 'Donald' had to be 17 units from another one, where a unit was one twelfth of a mile (approx. one seventh of a kilometre) or one 50ft (approx. 15m) contour. We can assume that, however informally,

Munro used some similar formula concerning distance and height differential.

Over the years, various developments have conspired to prompt further amendments to the Tables, including metrication, improved surveying methods (most recently by satellite), and a desire on the part of each succeeding generation of editors to reduce what they have regarded as 'anomalies.' For example, the 'mountain range in miniature' of Beinn Eighe was awarded a second Munro in 1997 to redress the balance with similar but over-endowed multi-topped ridges such as the seven-Munro South Glen Shiel Ridge. Changes and the reasons for change are detailed individually in the main text (see Peak Fitness for details).

The first metric edition of the Tables in 1974 listed 279 Munros and 262 Tops. The 1981 edition listed 276 Munros and 240 Tops. The 1990 edition added an extra Munro. The current (1997) edition lists 284 Munros and 227 Tops. Watch this space.

BEIN IME

The first person to bag all the Munros may have been the Rev Archibald Robertson in 1901, although his notebooks bear no mention of him having climbed the Inaccessible Pinnacle and note that he gave up on Ben Wyvis to avoid a wetting.

The second Munroist was the Rev Ronald Burn, who additionally bagged all the Tops, in 1923, thus becoming the first 'Compleat Munroist' or Compleater. The third was James Parker, who additionally bagged all the Tops and Furths (the 3000ft summits of England, Wales and Ireland), in 1929. The latest edition of the Tables lists 1745 known Munroists.

THE SCOTTISH HIGHLANDS

The Scottish Highlands are characterised by a patchwork of mountains separated by deep glens, the result of glacial erosion in the distant past. On a global scale the mountains reach an insignificant height, topping out at (1344m/4409ft) on Ben Nevis. But in form they hold their own against any range in the world, many rising bold and beautiful from sea-level. For hillwalkers they

BEN VORLICH

have distinct advantages over higher mountain ranges: their height is ideal for day walks and glens give easy road access.

Moreover, the variety of mountain forms and landscapes is arguably greater than in any mountainous area of equivalent size. This is due to many factors, notably differing regional geology and the influence of the sea.

In an attempt to give some order to this complexity, the Highlands are traditionally divided into six regions, as detailed below. The potted overviews mislead in that they mask the variety within each region, ignore numerous exceptions to the rule and reflect road access as much as discernible regional boundaries, but they serve as introductory descriptions.

The Southern Highlands 46 Munros	Gentle, green and accessible, with scope for a great variety of mountain walks.
The Central Highlands 73 Munros	A combination of all the other regions, with some of the greatest rock faces in the country.
The Cairngorms 50 Munros	Great rolling plateaus, vast corries, remote mountain sanctuaries, sub-arctic ambience.
The Western Highlands 63 Munros	Dramatic landscapes, endless seascapes, narrow ridges, arrowhead peaks, rugged terrain.
The Northern Highlands 39 Munros	Massive, monolithic mountains rising out of a desolate, watery wilderness.
The Islands 13 Munros	Exquisite mountainscapes, knife-edge ridges, sky-high scrambling, maritime ambience.

THE SOUTHERN HIGHLANDS

The region covered by this guidebook, as its name implies, is the most southerly region in the Scottish Highlands. It is bounded on the west by the sea, on the east by the Tay Valley (the A9 Perth – Pitlochry road) and on the north by a line that runs along the A85 from Oban to Tyndrum, up the A82 to Rannoch Moor, then eastwards along Loch Rannoch and Loch Tummel to Pitlochry. In the south it is bounded by the central belt of Scotland between Glasgow and Edinburgh, below which the Southern Uplands continue to the English border.

The region itself is divided into two distinct halves by a geological zone of fracture known as the Highland Boundary Fault, which runs in a straight line across the breadth of Scotland from south-west to north-east. From the west coast it crosses Loch Lomond at Balmaha, passes through the Trossachs at Aberfoyle and heads north-east through Glen Artney to the Tay Valley and beyond, eventually to reach the east coast at Stonehaven.

Although the fault is hundreds of millions of years old, tremors are still felt along it as the rocks continue to settle, making the town of Crieff the earthquake capital of the British Isles.

South of the Highland Boundary Fault lie green rounded hills, while north of it lie rougher mountains, including all the region's 46 Munros and accompanying 21 Tops, to say nothing of 36 Corbetts. The rocks are mostly sedimentary but they have been greatly metamorphosed, uplifted and folded over time. Rolling folds parallel to the Highland Boundary Fault have rippled the land into Munro-height mountains separated by deep depressions, of which the largest is the great strath that runs from Crianlarich through Glen Dochart to Killin, then along Loch Tay to Aberfeldy and Pitlochry.

Although the ground to the north of the fault is rougher than that to the south, it is nowhere near as rugged as further north and west in the Highlands, while the igneous Cairngorm plateaus to the east are different again. The Southern Highland landscape is more gentle, more rounded and more verdant, though with enough geological variation and Ice Age sculpting to include an occasional rock playground for climbers and scramblers. Examples include the overhanging rock faces of The Cobbler, the great Prow of Stuc a' Chroin and the craggy corries of the Bridge of Orchy mountains.

Apart from some notable exceptions, the Munros cluster in groups separated by lochs and deep glens, which carry an extensive road system that eases access. Within each group the Munros are often close enough together to make multi-bagging trips practicable. The region therefore has the best of both worlds. Its Munros are easily accessible

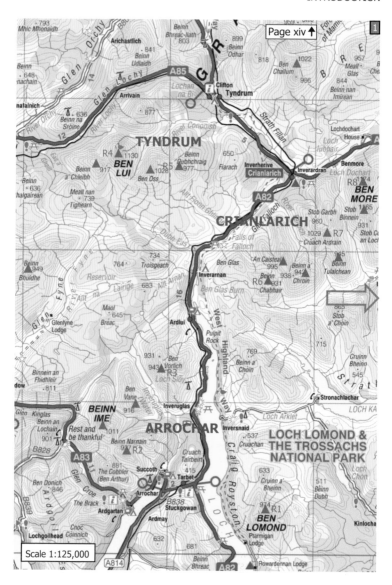

Page xiv ↑

Scale 1:125,000

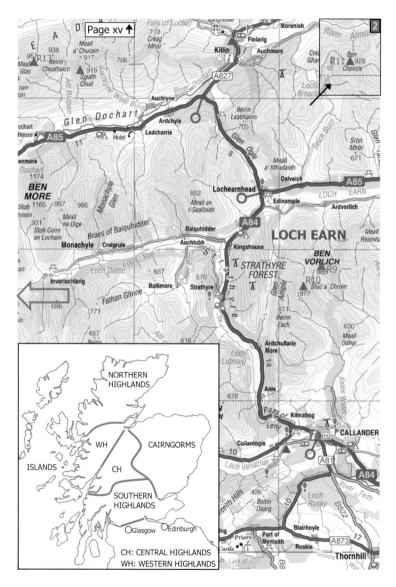

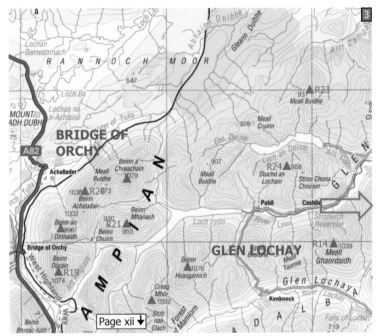

individually, while their clustering facilitates combined ascents.

Of the 46 Munros shown on the accompanying maps, this guidebook describes easy routes up 25 of them (marked R1–R25), carefully selected to showcase a cross-section of Southern Highland geography and mountain form. They are described in roughly west-to-east and south-to-north order. For dual bagging trips an additional 9

easy neighbouring Munros are described as 'Bonus Munros' for the sufficiently fit and enthusiastic.

There are, of course, more demanding Southern Highland Munros to climb, some of which require the crossing of steep, unstable ground, narrow and exposed ridges and rocky terrain. Similarly, there are more demanding routes up the easy Munros described herein. If you want to

Let's get one thing straight: taking the easy way up a Munro does not diminish your hillwalking credentials. Just because you have your mind set on higher matters than groping rock all day doesn't mean you have to hang up your boots and go lie on a beach. The joys of hillwalking are not circumscribed by the difficulty of the endeavour. Sir Hugh himself was perfectly happy to take an easy way up a mountain if there was one and there's no reason you shouldn't follow in his footsteps.

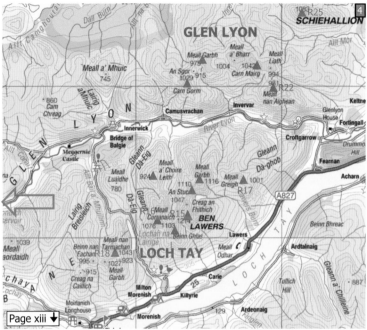

Page xiii ↓

explore further or know everything there is to know about *all* the Southern Highland Munros, consult volume 1 of our sister series *The Ultimate Guide to the Munros*.

As the nearest region to the most populated parts of Scotland, the Southern Highlands contain many of the country's most popular Munros. Only the Central Highlands' Ben Nevis, the highest in the land, is climbed more times than Ben Lomond, the centrepiece of Scotland's first National Park, created in 2002. Other popular mountains include Loch Earn's Ben Vorlich (one of the nearest to Edinburgh), historic Schiehallion and

Ben Lawers (reached by a road that climbs to a height of 550m/1800ft). The shortest route in this book bags a Munro for a mere 520m/1700ft of ascent, but what a viewpoint it is! (Meall Buidhe – Route 23).

If you're new to the Scottish Highlands, the Southern Highlands are a great place to start: easy access, a variety of mountains, a whole host of different routes, extensive views over deep glens and ribbon lochs… and, with the aid of this guidebook, no less than 25+ easy Munros to bag.

Memo to self: What are you waiting for? Get your boots on!

SEASONS AND WEATHER

From a hillwalking perspective, the Highland year has two seasons: the snow season and the no-snow season. The length of these seasons varies from year to year and from place to place.

From May to September, snow is rarely a problem. Historically, May and June have the greatest number of sunny days, with the air at its clearest. July and August are the hottest months but are also more prone to rain and haze, not to mention that blight on the landscape, the Highland midge. The biting season begins in mid to late June and lasts until the first chills of late September. By October it is colder, the hills get their first dusting of winter snow and good days are few and far between.

The months from November to April, though sometimes earlier and later, are characterised by short days, cold and snow. March and April are transition months, with little or lots of snow. In some years, snow can last into early summer and be a nuisance on some routes. If you are unequipped for it, turn back. Snow is more treacherous to descend than ascend, and spring snow often has a crystalline quality that makes it behave like ball-bearings.

In a normal winter (whatever that is, these days), conditions vary from British to Alpine to Arctic. An easy summer route can be made life-threatening by icy conditions and severe winter weather. When paths are obliterated by snow, hillsides become treacherous and walking becomes difficult and tiring.

On a clear winter's day the Scottish mountains have an Alpine quality that makes for unforgettable days out, but no-one should attempt a Munro in winter without adequate clothing and equipment (including ice-axe and crampons), and experience (or the company of an experienced person). The number of accidents, some of them fatal, that occur in the Highlands every winter should leave no doubt as to the need for caution.

MEALL CORRANAICH

Sample weather forecasts:
www.metoffice.gov.uk/loutdoor/
    mountainsafety/ Tel: West (09068-
    500442), East (09068-500441)
www.metcheck.com/V40/UK/HOBBIES/
    mountain.asp   www.mwis.org.uk
www.sais.gov.uk (avalanche conditions)

Webcams may be available for specific mountain areas. Try a web search. Useful webcams at the time of writing, though in the Central rather than Southern Highlands: http://trafficscotland.org/lev/index.aspx (A9 east) and www.kingy.com (Glen Coe west).

USING THIS BOOK

Position in Munro's Tables
(1 = highest)

OS 1:50,000
map number

Grid reference

▲**Ben Lomond** 179 974m/3195ft (OS 56, NN 367028)
Beacon Mountain, from the Gaelic *laom*

Many Munro names are Gaelic in origin. We give approximate pronunciations but make no claim to definitiveness. For example, the correct pronunciation of Ben is akin to *Pyne*, with a soft *n* as in the first syllable of *onion*, but it would be pedantic to enforce a purist pronunciation on a non-Gaelic speaker. The name Bealach, meaning Pass, is pronounced *byalach*, but many find it hard not to call it a *beelach*. And if you're one of those unfortunates who appear congenitally incapable of pronouncing *loch* as anything other than *lock*, you're in trouble.

In connection with the phonetic pronunciations given, note that Y before a vowel is pronounced as in *you*, OW is pronounced as in *town* and CH is pronounced as in Scottish *loch* or German *noch.*

Meall Buidhe from Loch an Daimh
NN 512464, 5½ml/9km, 520m/1700ft

The maps used in this book are reproductions of OS 1:50,000 maps at 75% full size (i.e. 1:66,667 or 1.5cm per 1km).

Route distances are specified in miles (to the nearest half-mile) and kilometres (to the nearest kilometre). Short distances are specified in metres (an approximate imperial measurement is yards). Total amount of ascent for a route is specified to the nearest 10m (50ft) and should be regarded as an approximation only.

To calculate how long a route will take, many begin with Naismith's Rule (one hour per 3ml/5km + half-hour per 1000ft/300m). This can be adjusted by an appropriate factor to suit your own pace and to cater for stoppages, foul weather, technical difficulty, rough terrain, tiredness and decrepitude. (Bill Naismith, 1856–1935, was the 'father' of the SMC.)

River directions, left bank and right bank, refer to the downstream direction. When referring to the direction of travel, we specify left-hand and right-hand.

The symbols ▲ and Δ indicate Munros and Tops respectively. An ATV track is an All-Terrain Vehicle track, rougher than a Land Rover track.

ACCESS

L and access was revolutionised by The Land Reform (Scotland) Act 2003 and the accompanying Scottish Outdoor Access Code (2005), which created a statutory right of responsible access for outdoor recreation. It is recommended that anyone walking in the Scottish countryside familiarise himself/herself with the Code, which explains rights and responsibilities in detail. Further information: www.outdooraccess-scotland.com.

Deer stalking considerations: Most of the Scottish Highlands are privately owned and non-compliance with stalking restrictions is likely to be counter-productive and cause aggravation for all concerned. If revenue is lost because of interference with stalking activities, estates may be forced to turn to afforestation or worse, thereby increasing access problems.

The red stag stalking season runs from July 1 to October 20 but actual dates vary from locality to locality. Access notices dot the roadside and information on stalking activities can be obtained from estate offices and head stalkers.

An increasing number of estates contribute to the Hillphones service, which provides daily recorded messages of where stalking is taking place. Further information can be found on the Outdoor Access website or on the Hillphones website: www.hillphones.info. Alternatively, leaflets can be obtained from The Mountaineering Council of Scotland, The Old Granary, Perth PH1 5QP.

It is worth noting that there is no stalking on a Sunday and that land belonging to public bodies such as the National Trust for Scotland and the John Muir Trust is normally not subject to stalking restrictions. See main text for specific access considerations.

TERRAIN

M ost of the standard Munro ascent routes have been boot-worn into paths and in some cases beyond that into ribbons of bog. In general, they have little in common with the kind of manicured paths found in the Alps or the Furth of Scotland (England and Wales).

Path restoration programmes began some years ago and continue apace, such that many popular routes now boast excellent renovated paths. At the other extreme some paths have degenerated into quagmires. Be prepared always for rough, rugged terrain and wear appropriate footwear.

The new Schiehallion path

▲Ben Lomond 179 974m/3195ft (OS 56, NN 367028)
Beacon Mountain, from the Gaelic *laom*

In olden times, the complex geography of the Highlands and the closed nature of clan society made cross-country communication difficult. When it was necessary to gather people together, e.g. to summon men to arms or warn of approaching danger (from the Romans or Vikings, perhaps, or even the English!), fires were raised on prominent hills such as Ben Lomond, hence its name.

S econd only to Ben Nevis in popularity, this most southerly of all Munros is nowhere near as great a mountain, yet it has undeniable presence. Standing in splendid isolation, it shows up as a shapely cone from some angles, and it certainly occupies a prime site above its famously picturesque loch.

The Tourist Path to the summit, complete with man-made rock staircases in places, was renovated in the 1990s at a cost of £340,000. It now offers both a straightforward ascent route and an unrivalled opportunity to assess at first hand the merits (or otherwise) of modern path maintenance schemes.

The roads and villages around Loch Lomond, on both sides of the loch and in nearby Arrochar, boast one of the best tea-shop crawls in the Scottish Highlands. With judicious timing, Ben Lomond can be climbed between refreshment stops.

Ben Lomond from Rowardennan: The Tourist Path
NS 360986, 8ml/12km, 1000m/3300ft

Some traditionalists may find Ben Lomond today a tad too brow-beaten for their tastes, but the ascent route merits top marks for its ease and viewsomeness. The path begins inauspiciously behind the toilet block at Rowardennan car park, at the end of the road along the east side of Loch Lomond. Once you've found the toilet block, directions are superfluous. Just follow the person in front of you! Even if you find yourself in the newsworthy position of having the mountain to yourself, the path is unmistakable.

BEN LOMOND

Ptarmigan   NW Ridge   S Ridge

Loch Lomond

It first climbs through the forestry plantation that surrounds Rowardennan. After reaching open hillside it continues up grassy slopes to Sron Aonaich (*Strawn Ernich*, Nose of the Ridge, 577m/1893ft), where the angle eases at the start of Ben Lomond's broad south ridge. The summit looks disappointingly dull from here, like a great flattened pudding, but appearances are deceptive. The skyline is the lip of Coire a' Bhathaich (*Corra Vah-ich*, Corrie of the Byre), a craggy corrie hidden on the north side of the mountain (and whose name is misleadingly placed on the OS map).

For a novel approach, reach Rowardennan, on the east side of Loch Lomond, from Inverbeg, on the A82 along the west side. A ferry runs from Easter to October. It leaves Inverbeg at 10.30, 14.30 and 18.30, and Rowardennan at 10.00, 14.00 and 17.30. Enquiries: Rowardennan Hotel (tel: 01360-870273).

The path up Sron Aonaich

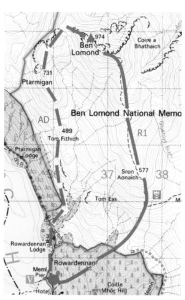

The path rises gently up the south ridge before climbing more steeply, though still easily, to the corrie lip. Here the craggy corrie walls suddenly drop away beneath your feet, seeming doubly dramatic after the mountain's gentle southern slopes. The path continues along the corrie rim to the cliff-top ▲summit.

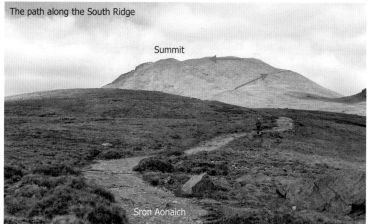

The path along the South Ridge

Summit

Sron Aonaich

If you're feeling energetic... the Ben Lomond Race record (up and down from Rowardennan Hotel) stands at just over one hour. (This is not a misprint.)

Alternative Descent: Ptarmigan

For negligible extra mileage and ascent, you can return over the subsidiary peak of Ptarmigan to make a round trip that gives close-up views of Loch Lomond. The path is not as finely constructed as the Tourist Path but has nevertheless been renovated to an excellent standard. Be advised, however, that it threads an enjoyably intricate and in places rocky descent route that is by no means the leisurely 'afternoon stroll' of the Tourist Path.

First you must descend Ben Lomond's steep north-west ridge. The stony path makes light of it, but there are two short rocky sections that require a spot of easy handwork. If you can manage the first, immediately below the summit, you should have no problems further down. Below the second rocky section, which is hidden from sight just below the first, the path winds its way invitingly down to and along Ptarmigan's undulating summit ridge.

After passing a hidden lochan, the scenic descent from the end of the ridge, with Loch Lomond and its mosaic of islands spread out before you, is the equal of any in the Highlands. The path reaches the lochside at a forest track that is part of the West Highland Way and which will take you back to Rowardennan.

Descending Ben Lomond's NW Ridge

▲**Beinn Narnain** 259 926m/3038ft (OS 56, NN 271066)
Meaning obscure. Perhaps Mountain of the Notches (*Ben Vyarnan*, from aspirated Gaelic *bearn*) or Mountain of the Alders (*Ben Yarnan*, from aspirated Gaelic *fearn*)

▲**Beinn Ime** 118 1011m/3316ft (OS 56, NN 255084)
Ben Eema, Butter Mountain (butter was once made at shielings in its corries)

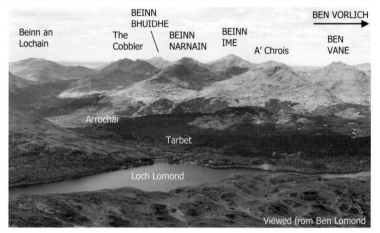

Viewed from Ben Lomond

The Arrochar Alps are a small group of rugged mountains, including four Munros, that tower over the village of Arrochar at the head of Loch Long, just west of Loch Lomond. Their grandiose title owes more to alliterative endeavour than topographical reality, but they deserve the accolade if only for their *pièce de résistance*: the remarkable rock peak of The Cobbler, perhaps the most eye-catching mountain in Scotland (although ironically not a Munro).

Apart from The Cobbler, the other peaks conceal their best features when viewed from the lochside. Beinn Ime, for instance, hides behind Beinn Narnain, whose summit is itself hidden behind dull convex slopes.

Fortunately the ascent of Narnain is more interesting than its initial appearance suggests, with a wonderful new approach path that was built at a cost of £300,000 in the 2000s. This gives ready access to the bealach between Narnain and Ime for a final ascent of under 300m/1000ft to the scenic cliff-top summit.

Nearby Beinn Ime is an equally easy add-on ascent from the bealach.

Beinn Narnain from Loch Long
NN 294049, 7ml/11km, 920m/3000ft

The route begins just beyond the turn-off to Succoth on the A83 at the head of Loch Long, just outside Arrochar. Opposite the car park (small parking fee payable at machine), the new path begins a convoluted climb up the hillside, trending left into the glen of the Allt a' Bhalachain (*Owlt a Valachin*, Buttermilk Burn) between The Cobbler and Beinn Narnain. Viewed from the lochside, the path's first objective is the low point seen on the skyline at NN 280051, where the stream is dammed.

The Cobbler   BEINN NARNAIN

Loch Long

The path first zigzags up to a forest road. Following red waymarks on posts, turn left, then right again beside a radio mast after c.60m, to follow a continuing Land Rover track up beside the Allt a' Bhalachain to the dam.

At the dam (marked as weir on OS map), ignore a side path that traverses right, back across the hillside, to the start of a steeper and rockier route up Beinn Narnain.

Beyond the dam the path runs beside the stream. On the right is the craggy south-west hillside of Beinn Narnain, but for the moment it is the view ahead, of The Cobbler's three rocky summits, that will rivet the attention. Soon you'll pass two giant rocks known as the Narnain Boulders, which were once a famous howff (natural shelter) used by early twentieth century rock climbers.

A swift descent beside the Allt a' Bhalachain

Further up you'll pass a junction where the path up The Cobbler bears left across the stream, while the main path continues to the bealach between The Cobbler and Beinn Narnain.

The new path ends here and a boggier path bears right across the hillside to the 637m/2090ft Bealach a' Mhaim (*Byalach a Vaa-im*, Pass of the Moor) between Narnain and Ime. Once you've reached the stile in the fence that crosses the bealach, all that separates you from Narnain's summit is a grassy 289m/948ft hillside.

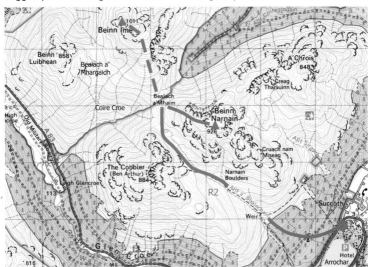

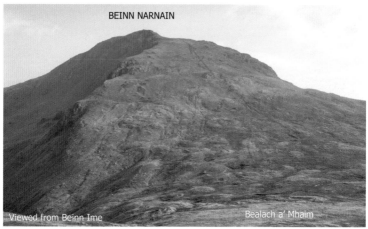

BEINN NARNAIN

Viewed from Beinn Ime   Bealach a' Mhaim

The path up the hillside is indistinct lower down and eroded higher up, although the line to take is obvious even if you lose the path. The standard route to the summit plateau goes straight up the hillside and across a boulderfield, where care is required to avoid a twisted ankle. To avoid the boulders, look for a path that bears right around them to reach the plateau further along, at the summit.

There are three substantial cairns on the summit plateau. The standard route arrives at the cairn at the plateau's near (north) end. From here a short stroll leads to the trig. pillar ▲summit and, just beyond, the centre cairn, where the indistinct boulderfield-avoiding path arrives from the right. Further along, at the south end of the plateau, is another cairn that marks the top of The Spearhead.

BEN LOMOND

Loch Lomond (somewhere)

The Spearhead

The south end of Beinn Narnain's summit plateau comes to an abrupt halt at the 25m/60ft rock fang known as The Spearhead. Beside it, beneath the summit, lies a shelf of giant jumbled boulders. If you enjoy scrambling, this can be reached (with care) and explored (with care), as long as you take even more care not to fall into assorted cave-like holes in the ground.

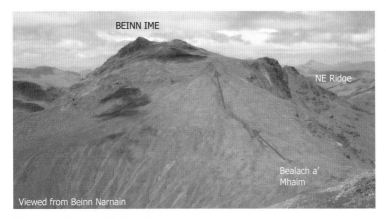

BEINN IME

NE Ridge

Bealach a' Mhaim

Viewed from Beinn Narnain

Bonus Munro: Beinn Ime add-on 2ml/3km, 380m/1250ft

After returning to the Bealach a' Mhaim, the ascent of Beinn Ime is little more than a 374m/1227ft aerobic workout on uniform grass slopes. The path is eroded and quite boggy at first but, after reaching a small plateau at the junction with the north-east ridge, it becomes rockier and firmer for the final push to the rocky nipple of a ▲summit.

After returning to the Bealach a' Mhaim again, bear right to follow the boggy path back across the hillside to the Narnain–Cobbler bealach, where you'll rejoin the approach path for a swift jog back down to the car park.

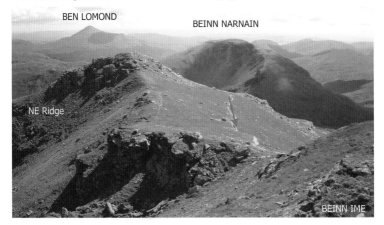

BEN LOMOND

BEINN NARNAIN

NE Ridge

BEINN IME

▲Ben Vorlich 229 943m/3094ft (OS 56, NN 295124)

The meaning is a problem. The *Vor* part could derive from the aspirated Gaelic *Mur* (Wall), *Muir* (Sea) or *Mor* (Big). The *lich* part could derive from an even greater variety of Gaelic words. The name is often translated as Mountain of the Sea-bag or Bag-shaped Bay (from *Muir-bhalg*), but equally possible are Big Mountain (from *Mhor-thulaich*) and Mountain of the Moor of the Hollow (from *Mhur-luig*). There's also another possibility: *Mhuirlaich* means kingfisher.

BEN VORLICH

Coire na Baintighearna

Loch Sloy

Ardlui

Inveruglas

Loch Lomond

Viewed from Ben Lomond

Towering over the northern reaches of Loch Lomond, the sprawling mass of Ben Vorlich covers about as much ground as all the other Arrochar Munros combined. It is separated from them by the trench of Loch Sloy to the west and boasts its own brand of hillwalking on three panoramic ridges that jut north-east, east and south-east above Loch Lomond.

The middle (east) ridge climbs over two steep cones known as the Little Hills to divide the Lomond side of the mountain into two great corries: the southern Coire na Baintighearna (*Ben-tyurna*, Lady) and the northern Coire Creagach (*Craikach*, Craggy). The south-east ridge, which rises around the south side of Coire na Baintighearna, gives a pleasant enough ascent, yet it can hardly be recommended over the north-east ridge, which rises around the north side of Coire Creagach.

This latter ridge has the benefit of an approach path that makes it the standard ascent route on the mountain, with great views over Loch Lomond. The only drawback is that it can be infuriatingly boggy after rain, so leave the ascent for a dry spell.

Ben Vorlich from Ardlui (Loch Lomond)
NN 319151, 6ml/10km, 980m/3200ft

The path to the mountain begins on the A82 at the north end of Loch Lomond, at the *second* railway underpass south of and 300m from Ardlui railway station. Park in the lay-by opposite the station. Walk along the often busy road with care and go through the underpass to leave the traffic behind.

The path rises diagonally across the hillside and climbs uniform slopes of grass and bracken to a small dam high up in Coire Creagach (NN 308139). The dam is on the first stream that comes down from the saddle on the north-east ridge.

Leave the path here (it soon ends anyway) and follow the stream up the grassy hillside to the saddle, situated between Ben Vorlich's North Top and Stob nan Coinnich Bhacain (*Stop nan Coan-yich Vach-kan*, poss. Peak of the Mossy Notch). There is currently no path on this stretch, so choose your own line to find the best going.

The north-east ridge climbs from the saddle to the North Top, becoming increasingly rocky with height. For a spot of easy scrambling, stay left near the rim of Coire Creagach, otherwise keep right on a path that finds easier going on more broken slopes.

The Little Hills
2   1
BEN VORLICH
Coire Creagach
Loch Lomond
Ardlui

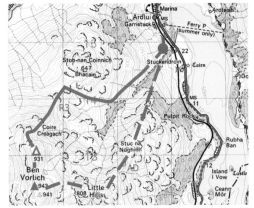

Once you've reached the ΔNorth Top, a short, very pleasant sky-high stroll across a shallow saddle is all that separates you from the ▲summit cairn.

Before leaving the summit area, take time to stroll across the next shallow dip to the south, where a trig. pillar stands atop a small rise. From here you'll get an eagle's eye view of the vast, island-studded southern reaches of Loch Lomond.

Alternative Descent: The Little Hills add-on 190m/600ft

The middle (east) ridge on Vorlich's Lomond side divides the mountain into its two great eastern corries and sports goodly amounts of rock on its abrupt twin tops – the two Little Hills. A return over these misleadingly named protuberances adds some spice to the return trip.

There are some steep, pathless sections, including the initial descent from the summit, and some hidden

tiers of cliffs whose avoidance makes for 'entertaining' route-finding. You'll also eventually have to cross the river that flows out of the deep-cut glen below Coire Creagach, to rejoin the approach path further down, so don't attempt this return route unless you're prepared to tackle with humour every obstacle it puts in your way.

Your reward? Stunning close-up views over Loch Lomond.

▲ **Ben Lui** 28 1130m/3707ft (OS 50, NN 266263)
Ben Loo-y, Calf Mountain (from Gaelic *Laoigh*) or Lead Mountain
(from Gaelic *Luaidhe*). Both meanings have claim, although the
mountain was named before Tyndrum became a lead mining village
in the eighteenth century. Some profess to see the shape of a horned
calf in Lui's twin summits, but the name Calf Mountain most likely
derives from times when cattle were a mainstay of clan life.
▲**Beinn a' Chleibh** 281 916m/3005ft (OS 50, NN 250256)
Ben a Chlave, Mountain of the Creel or Basket

BEN LUI

Summit   NW Top

Central
Gully

Coire
Gaothach

Ben Lui 'in winter raiment'
viewed from Dalrigh

North of the Arrochar Alps and
west of the A82 Crianlarich–
Tyndrum road, half-hidden behind
lower hills, a twisting east-west line
of four Munros forms one of the most
distinctive mountain groups in the
Southern Highlands.

Ben Lui, the highest of the four
peaks, is one dramatic mountain,
of such character that it begs to be
climbed. Take one glance at its
northern slopes from near Dalrigh,
east of Tyndrum, and you'll be
hooked. Its height, symmetry and

isolation, especially when seen 'in winter raiment' (as old-style guide-books used to say), give it a positively Himalayan grandeur. We kid you not.

The Munro larges it over its hinterland at the end of lengthy Glen Cononish, sporting airy twin tops that drop steep ridges to enclose Coire Gaothach (*Corra Geu-ich*, Windy Corrie). From the bowl of the corrie, Central Gully rises to the skyline between the two tops. An approach

from Dalrigh and an ascent via the bounding arms of Coire Gaothach, up one and down the other, is a classic Southern Highland scramble.

Fortunately, for non-seekers of an adrenaline rush, the peak's western slopes offer an easy way up the 'back side' of the mountain. From this direction also the route offers an easy add-on stroll up the adjacent satellite Munro of Beinn a' Chleibh, giving you an extra Munro for your efforts.

BEN LUI

Coire Gaothach

Viewed from Ben Oss

A good time to visit Ben Lui is late spring or early summer, after snow has left the mountain's western slopes but still blankets north-facing Coire Gaothach. In a good winter, a mighty cornice forms at the deeply incised head of the corrie's Central Gully. Take care near the lip to avoid inadvertently stepping over the abyss.

The floor of the corrie is often carpeted with avalanche debris from the cornice. The ascent of the gully by members of the newly formed Scottish Mountaineering Club in 1891 traditionally marks the beginning of winter climbing in the Highlands.

Ben Lui from Glen Lochy
Ben Lui: NN 239278, 5ml/8km, 940m/3100ft

On their west sides, the summits of Ben Lui and Beinn a' Chleibh enclose the deep green bowl of Fionn Choirein (*Fyoon Chorran*, White Corrie). The corrie's main stream flows into another stream, confusingly named Eas Daimh (*Aiss Daff*, Stag Waterfall), which eventually enters the River Lochy in Glen

The ford of the River Lochy

Lochy. Near the confluence with the Lochy, 6½ml/10km west of Tyndrum on the A85 through the glen, the route begins at a Munro baggers' car park.

Both Munros rise stoutly out of the forest above the car park. Lui's north-west top appears as a steep pyramid, hiding the true summit. Chleibh appears as a bold grassy dome encrusted with crags above Fionn Choirein. The forest and crags dictate that the only practicable route up Chleibh is via the corrie and the bealach between the two Munros.

BEN LUI

NW Ridge

Eas Daimh

Separating car park from open ground is a variety of obstacles: the River Lochy, the West Highland Railway line and blanket forest. A path runs down to the river and along the bank to the confluence with the Eas Daimh. Unless the water is very low, the only way to cross the River Lochy is to paddle.

Tip: Carry your boots from the car park down to the River Lochy and paddle across it in old trainers, then boot up and leave your trainers on the near bank for the return crossing.

N.B. There is a footbridge about ½ml/1km downriver at NN 229271, but using it would necessitate a frustrating detour and an illegal walk back along the railway line.

On the far bank of the river, the railway line bridges the Eas Daimh. Paddle under the bridge (it is illegal to cross the line) to find a well-worn path along the left-hand (north) bank of the Eas Daimh between forest and stream. Don't just put your head down and walk or you'll miss an important path fork after c.400m, where the tributary stream coming down from Fionn

Choirein leaps into the Eas Daimh at a small waterfall.

While the left-hand path continues along the Eas Daimh, the right-hand path heads for Ben Lui, crossing the Eas Daimh on stepping stones and climbing the left-hand side of the tributary stream all the way to the upper forest fence (NN 249266) and into Fionn Choirein.

Like most paths of its ilk, it is 'amusingly boggy' in parts. That said, it is nowhere near as glutinous as the Beinn Dubhchraig path (Route 5), while numerous small cascades offer distraction. N.B. At the time of writing, the Forestry Commission hopes to upgrade the whole route.

After exiting the forest at the 470m/1550ft contour, you find yourself in the bowl of Fionn Choirein, where the going improves dramatically. There's even a large wooden monolith, like something out of the film *2001*, to welcome you to Ben Lui National Nature Reserve.

To the left, grassy slopes rise to Ben Lui's north-west ridge. To the right is the precipitous north-east face of Beinn a' Chleibh. On the skyline ahead is the bealach between the two Munros.

The path in upper Fionn Chorein

The improved path continues up beside the stream into the upper corrie. To avoid steep terrain, it doesn't head directly for the bealach but instead climbs well left beside a minor stream before cutting back right across easier ground. It becomes indistinct on wet ground in the upper corrie but improves again to make the final diagonal climb up to the bealach.

On the bealach itself, the path splits – left to Lui and right to Chleibh. The 370m/1200ft climb up Lui's south-west shoulder begins well on grass and rocks but deteriorates higher up on steep, stony ground that requires determination.

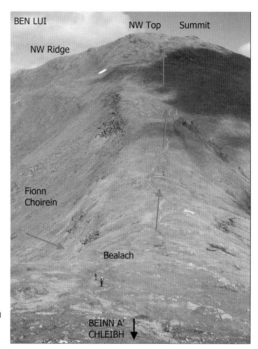

BEN LUI   NW Top   Summit
NW Ridge
Fionn Choirein
Bealach
BEINN A' CHLEIBH

The summit of Ben Lui

Central Gully

The path emerges onto the skyline at the dip between the twin tops, with the abyss of Coire Gaothach suddenly beneath your feet. Go left to the north-west top then right to the 3m/10ft higher chunk of rock that forms the castellated ▲summit. You'll want to spend some time here.

Looking down the SE Arm Of Coire Gaothach

Coire Gaothach

Bonus Munro: Beinn a' Chleibh add-on 1ml/2km, 160m/500ft

After returning to the bealach, you'll find Beinn a' Chleibh so easy to bag that you'll almost begrudge its status as a Munro. Surely they shouldn't be this easy?

To reach the flat ▲summit simply follow the obvious path 160m/500ft up the broad, grassy north-east ridge. Once up, you may wish to take a stroll north-west across the summit plateau, following cairns, for an uninterrupted view of Ben Cruachan and the other Munros around Loch Awe.

When you're ready, return to the bealach once again... and look forward with renewed vigour to that fun re-descent through the forest and ford of the River Lochy.

BEINN A' CHLEIBH

Bealach

Fionn Choirein

Viewed from Ben Lui

▲Beinn Dubhchraig 175 978m/3209ft (OS 50, NN 307254)
Ben Doo-chraik, Black Crag Mountain

BEN OSS   BEINN DUBHCHRAIG

Viewed from the south

When travelling along the A82 from Crianlarich to Tyndrum, you may be forgiven for not giving Beinn Dubhchraig a second glance. That squashed pudding of a hill lurking in the shadow of majestic Ben Lui (Route 4) can't be a Munro, can it? Indeed it can. You're looking at the mountain-out-of-a-molehill that is Beinn Dubhchraig. To its immediate west and barely more exciting, Ben Oss cowers sheepishly behind it, equally overawed by Lui's presence.

The duo's best features lie on their hidden south side, where their connecting ridge, fringed by crags, forms a horseshoe around remote Loch Oss. Unfortunately the walk-in to the loch is long, featureless and pathless, and can scarcely be

recommended over the northern approach from Dalrigh near Tyndrum.

From here the ascent of Beinn Dubhchraig is technically as easy as they come, but there's a drawback. We're talking bog. Not just any old bog. We're talking Slough of Despond. After rain the going as far as the tree line is execrable. Until the approach path is replaced by an escalator, you may prefer to leave the ascent for a drought.

If you survive the forest without getting sucked down, the remainder of the route makes an enjoyable skyline circuit of Coire Dubhchraig, crossing the summit as it does so. And you can even avoid the bog on the way back down (see Alternative Descent on Page 23).

Tyndrum (*Tyne-drum*, not *Tindrum*, from the Gaelic *Tigh an Druim*) means House on the Ridge. Dalrigh (*Dal-ree*, from the Gaelic *Dal Righ*) means King's Field. During his long campaign to impose himself as King of

Scotland, Robert Bruce fought the MacDougalls of Lorn here in 1306. And lost.

He didn't get his own back until a rematch on the slopes of Ben Cruachan two years later.

Beinn Dubhchraig from Dalrigh
NN 344291, 7½ml/12km, 800m/2600ft

Begin at Dalrigh car park, just off the A82 2ml/3km east of Tyndrum. Steps at the far end of the car park descend to a road that leads to a bridge over the River Cononish. On the far side of the bridge, turn immediately right on a Land Rover track that leads to a bridge over the West Highland Railway line at NN 336285.

On the far side of the railway bridge, a boggy path branches right to a footbridge over the Allt Gleann Auchreoch at NN 333284. You can avoid the boggy going by continuing up the track to a left-hand bend, from where drier paths lead back down to the footbridge. On the other hand, you might as well accustom yourself to the boggy stuff now.

On the far side of the footbridge, a path goes up the right-hand side of the Allt Gleann Auchreoch and then the right-hand side of the Allt Coire Dubhchraig, climbing all the way through Coire Dubhchraig to two lochans on Beinn Dubhchraig's north-west ridge. We trust your boots are waterproof and advise you to pack a snorkel. If you want to detour around the worst of the bog, check out the Alternative Descent on Page 23.

The sodden path passes through the beautiful old pine forest of Coille Coire Chuilc (*Cull-ya Corra Cool-ak*, Wood of the Reedy Corrie), although, conditions being as they are, you may find its beautiful oldness hard to appreciate. You may find it even harder to understand how Dubhchraig acquired its imposing name (the 'black crag' is on the south side of the mountain).

BEINN DUBHCHRAIG

NE Ridge

NW Ridge

two lochans

Coire Dubhchraig

Viewed from near Dalrigh

The underfoot morass deteriorates still further as you leave the wood and climb through newer forestry plantations. When the trees finally begin to thin out at their upper boundary, don't let quagmires draw you away from the stream-side path as it makes its way into the vast open spaces of shallow Coire Dubhchraig.

BEN CHALLUM

The bog awaits

Here at last matters start to improve. The stream itself forms an attractive series of cascades as it drops over a long staircase of ledges. The path remains boggy in parts but feels like baked earth compared to what you've just negotiated.

Should you have made it this far, there is a choice of ways out of the corrie. Dubhchraig's summit is on the left, at the head of the easy north-east ridge, but the path follows the stream right to climb diagonally across the corrie to two skyline lochans at the junction of the north and north-west ridges. We suggest you make a round trip by going up the north-east ridge and down the corrie.

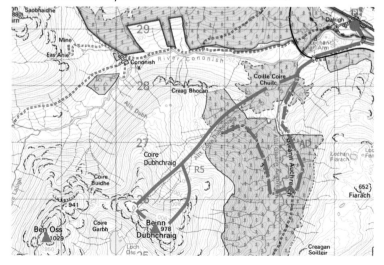

Cross the stream and bear left up grassy slopes to gain the broad ridge crest, which starts steeply but eases with height. There are no more than traces of path but the going is good on grass among boulders and the ridge-top views are much better than down in the corrie.

BEINN DUBHCHRAIG

NE Ridge

BEINN DUBHCHRAIG

NW Ridge

The gentle ▲summit is a pleasant and scenic spot that will, temporarily at least, expunge from memory all thoughts of the boggy approach path. Relax and enjoy the sublime view. To the south Loch Lomond curls around the foot of Ben Lomond, while to the west the ever more unlikely shark's fin of Ben Lui cleaves the air behind lumpy Ben Oss.

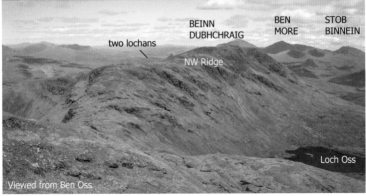

two lochans

BEINN DUBHCHRAIG

BEN MORE

STOB BINNEIN

NW Ridge

Loch Oss

Viewed from Ben Oss

Continuing the round of the corrie skyline, the broad north-west ridge descends at an easy angle in the direction of Ben Oss, with Ben Lui as a backdrop. The ridge carries an indistinct path that gives a pleasant stroll down to the two lochans noted above (an eerie spot in cloud). Turn right here to descend into Coire Dubhchraig, where you'll soon pick up the path on the left side of the stream. This has one steep section beside a waterfall before it eases lower down and rejoins the approach route.

NW Ridge

two lochans

Upper Coire Dubhchraig

Alternative Descent: add-on 2ml/3km

On descent it is unlikely that you will relish revisiting the Slough of Despond, so you'll need no urging to consider this alternative.

The Land Rover track that crosses the West Highland Railway line at the start of the route becomes a forest track that climbs almost all the way to the upper forest boundary in Coire Dubhchraig. It makes a long, sweeping, easy-angled ascent that adds a couple of miles to the ascent/descent, but you'll probably cover that extra distance anyway in order to

avoid bog on the time-dishonoured traditional route. Most people take the traditional route on ascent, but on descent it's surprising how those extra couple of miles suddenly don't seem to matter so much.

To find the track on descent, cross the Allt Coire Dubhchraig when you reach the upper forest fence, then follow the right bank down for a few hundred metres, to an indentation in the forest perimeter, where the track starts on open ground a short distance from the stream.

BEN OSS   BEN LUI

Viewed from Beinn Dubhchraig

Beinn Dubhchraig is often climbed in combination with Ben Oss, the next Munro to the west, from which it is separated by a deep bealach. However, the descent to the bealach from Dubhchraig is steep enough for hands to be useful in places and will not appeal to anyone seeking easy routes up Munros.

▲Beinn Chabhair 244 933m/3060ft (OS 50 or 56, NN 367179)
Ben Chav-ir, Antler Mountain

BEINN CHABHAIR

Viewed from An Caisteal

Beinn Chabhair is one of three Munros that together form the Glen Falloch Group, a compact trio of mountains that dominates Glen Falloch on the south-west side of Crianlarich. The group is in itself a sub-group of seven Munros that together form the Crianlarich Group and yield three routes in this guidebook.

With grassy lower slopes rising to crag-spattered upper slopes, the whole Glen Falloch Group offers extensive hillwalking with odd spots of excitement to add spice to ascents. If you're looking to avoid such spots, Beinn Chabhair is the one Munro of the trio that, unlike its companions An Caisteal and Beinn a' Chroin, provides an easy approach and ascent.

Viewed from Glen Falloch, the summit lies well hidden behind lower western slopes steep enough to host Ben Glas Falls, a series of cascades formed by the Ben Glas Burn as it tumbles 36m/120ft down the 'Devil's Staircase' (well seen from the roadside). The time-honoured ascent route beside the falls is now very steep and eroded, but there's a newer path that gives ready access to the glen above, where Lochan Beinn Chabhair nestles beneath the upper slopes of its namesake peak.

For variety (and more effort) you can return via the north-west ridge and the secret beauty spot of Lochan a' Chaisteal (see Alternative Descent on Page 28).

Beinn Chabhair from Glen Falloch
NN 326202, 9ml/14km, 940m/3100ft

The A82 crosses the River Falloch around 4½ml/7km south of Crianlarich, where a farm track leaves the roadside to give access to the western slopes of Beinn Chabhair. Keep left at a fork and, at a prominent tree only a couple of hundred metres from the roadside, fork left again on an ATV track (marked as a path on the OS map).

BEINN CHABHAIR

The wide-open upper glen

Ben Glas Burn

The track-cum-path avoids the steep western slopes down which Ben Glas Falls tumble by approaching from the north, making a surprisingly gentle ascent of the hillside to reach the Ben Glas Burn well above the falls. It joins the path up beside the stream from Beinglas farm at the 300m contour (NN 329182), at the entrance to the wide-open upper glen.

notch   Upper NW Ridge

BEINN CHABHAIR

Lochan Beinn Chabhair

The path continues along the streambank to Lochan Beinn Chabhair at the foot of Beinn Chabhair's upper slopes. It is something of a quagmire in places so a sense of humour will ease its passage, but overall it gives a pleasant enough streamside ramble through 'undemanding' scenery to the reedy lochan.

BEINN CHABHAIR

On the Upper NW Ridge

The nondescript summit of Beinn Chabhair now rises ahead, sporting an infinite variety of ascent routes on grassy slopes among crags. For the most straightforward way up, look to the left, where a boulder slope rises to a notch on the north-west ridge, between Meall nan Tarmachan (no, not the Meall nan Tarmachan of Route 18) and Beinn Chabhair.

Summit

Upper NW Ridge

Beinglas farm, situated on the West Highland Way at the foot of Beinn Chabhair, 6ml/10km south of Crianlarich and 1½ml/2km south of the start of this route, has a restaurant and shop, as well as rooms, 'wigwams' and camping facilities. Open all day and all year. Tel: 01301-704281. Website: www.beinglascampsite.co.uk. Email: beinglas.campsite@virgin.net.

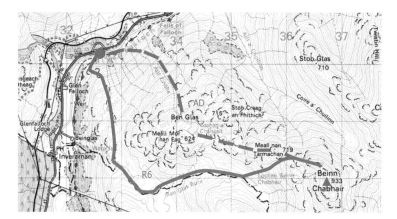

A path is developing on the right-hand side of the stream that descends from the notch. Follow it up then bear right up grassy slopes to gain the ridge itself. Once on the skyline, the path becomes well-defined and easy to follow as it twists its way upwards around outcrops. After reaching a subsidiary top, the ▲summit is only a short stroll away.

Looking back down the NW Ridge (Alternative Descent)

One of the best short walks in the area is to the wonderfully named Cnap Mor (*Crap Moar*, Big Knob), a 164m/538ft hillock situated 1½ml/2½km south of Beinglas farm along the West Highland Way.

The lowly summit offers a great view along Loch Lomond to Ben Lomond, and the best view from anywhere of Ben Vorlich (Route 3), seen across the marinas of Ardlui (picture on Page 11).

Alternative Descent: Lochan a' Chaisteil

add-on mileage and ascent: negligible; add-on effort: considerable

Left of the skyline notch above Lochan Beinn Chabhair, the lower north-west ridge of Beinn Chabhair is a confusing maze of knolls and unexpected drops. For anyone still suffering from a surfeit of energy at the summit, the descent of the ridge makes an adventurous return route past the little-known beauty spot of Lochan a' Chaisteal. This handsome lochan is encircled by castle-like crags (hence its name), which give it a rare air of seclusion high above the surrounding glens.

On descent from the summit of Beinn Chabhair, leave the path on approach to the notch and stay on the ridge. Go over Meall nan Tarmachan, descend steeper slopes to a dip on its far side and cross another rise. Ahead now is craggy Stob Creag an Fhithich (*Stop Craik an Ee-ich*, Peak of the Raven's Crag), which can be bypassed on the left to reach Lochan a' Chaisteal.

The lochan marks the end of the ridge but not the end of the adventure, as the steep hillside beyond, which separates you from the approach path, is beset with yet more knolls and crags. To avoid these, refrain from continuing in a north-west direction and attempting a direct line down. Instead, find the lochan's outlet stream (the Allt Criche, *Owlt Creecha*, Boundary Stream) and follow it down easier ground to the north.

Once below all difficulties, bear left across the easy-angled hillside to join the West Highland Way for a short stroll back beside the River Falloch to your starting point.

If you have time after descending from Beinn Chabhair, visit the Falls of Falloch, around one mile up the A82 towards Crianlarich (small car park). Although only c.9m/30ft high, their picturesque setting makes them worth the short trip.

▲**Cruach Ardrain** 87 1046m/3432ft (OS 51 or 56, NN 409212)
Croo-ach Aardran, High Mound
▲**Beinn Tulaichean** 220 946m/3104ft (OS 56, NN 416196)
Ben Toolichan, Knolly Mountain

Stob Garbh   CRUACH ARDRAIN   Grey Height

Cruach Ardrain is the most eye-catching of the seven Munros that form the Crianlarich Group. Its wedge-shaped summit towers over the forests of Coire Ardrain and looks particularly imposing when viewed in winter across the River Fillan. Access through the forest has been improved in recent years and the ascent to the cliff-edge summit is now both easy and interestingly intricate.

The adjacent Munro of Beinn Tulaichean, by contrast, is no more than the highpoint at the end of Ardrain's south-east ridge, requiring an ascent from the intervening bealach of only 121m/397ft. The ascent is an easy add-on to that of Ardrain.

In his original 1891 Tables, Sir Hugh guessed that Cruach Ardrain's NE top (NN 409212) was higher than its nearby SW top (NN 408211). However, his decision was based on map heights of 3477ft and 3429ft respectively. The '3477' was an erroneous guess on his part, as the first two digits were obliterated on his map, and it soon became obvious that the unreadable height was in fact '3377'. In 1921, therefore, despite the fact that the '3377' was plainly also incorrect, the SW top became the Munro. The situation was not rectified until 1981.

Cruach Ardrain from Crianlarich
NN 389251, 8ml/13km, 940m/3100ft

The route begins at the Community Woodland car park, situated at the east entrance to Crianlarich, and climbs the west rim of Coire Ardrain. Forest blankets the lower slopes to a height of nearly 500m/1650ft, but forest roads that climb to the upper boundary make access straightforward as long as you follow the detailed directions below.

Take the forest road into the woods, go right at the first junction after c.1000m (NN 386243) and left at the second after a further 400m (NN 384240). Just over 100m beyond the second junction, you'll cross the former, now horribly boggy, approach path from the A82.

Around 700m beyond the second junction, branch right at a third (NN 389237) and keep to this forest road even when it seems to be heading too far west. From its end at NN 383232, a boggy path makes a short climb to a horizontal forest ride. Open hillside now lies less than a couple of hundred metres to the right. Once outside the forest fence, follow it up to its highest point, where the old path comes in from the left over a stile.

Once above the forest, a distinct path climbs a more well-defined, grassy ridge to the Grey Height and continues across a broad saddle to the rocky top of Meall Dhamh (*Myowl Ghav*, Deer Hill).

Cruach Ardrain is awkwardly situated on the corners of no less than three maps. Both OS 50 and OS 51 are needed for its ascent, plus OS 56 if Beinn Tulaichean is to be included.

CRUACH ARDRAIN   SW Top   Summit   Stob Garbh   BEINN TULAICHEAN

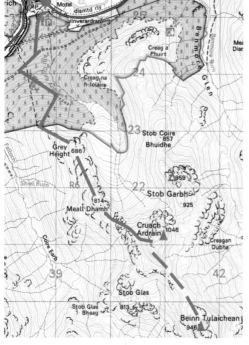

Beyond here the ridge becomes entertainingly intricate, forcing the path to negotiate a number of rocky knolls on a descent of around 50m/ 150ft to the foot of Cruach Ardrain's short sharp north-west ridge.

To overcome this final obstacle, the path takes a diagonal line up the grass slopes to the right of the ridge crest. These are quite steep but the going remains easy. The route passes beneath the summit to reach the skyline still further right, on the easy south-east ridge, just below the roof -like summit dome. To reach the true (north-east) ▲summit, cross a shallow dip beyond the first twin-cairned (south-west) top reached.

Bonus Munro: Beinn Tulaichean add-on 2½ml/4km, 350m/1150ft

Before you retrace steps to Crianlarich, the return jaunt to ▲Beinn Tulaichean will clock up another tick on the list for minimal effort. The well-trodden highway along Cruach Ardrain's south-east ridge descends steeply to the intervening bealach before making the short ascent to the ridge's end point at Tulaichean's knobbly summit.

CRUACH ARDRAIN

Y Gully

BEINN TULAICHEAN

Viewed from Cruach Ardrain

Anyone who has not had the foresight to purchase this guidebook could easily miss Beinn Tulaichean's most interesting feature. Just over (south of) the summit a landslip has created a warren of shafts and caves in a jumble of fissures and boulders. It is a curious phenomenon that is well worth a (careful) look.

▲Ben More 16 1174m/3852ft (OS 51, NN 432244)
Ben Moar, Big Mountain
▲Stob Binnein 18 1165m/3822ft (OS 51, NN 434227)
*Stop Beenyan (*usually pronounced *Stobinian)*, Conical Peak

STOB BINNEIN   BEN MORE

Loch Tay

East of Cruach Ardrain (Route 7) the commanding sentinels of Ben More and Stob Binnein tower above the dense forest that carpets Coire Chaorach (*Corra Cheurach*, Corrie of Rowan Berries). Ben More especially rears up in an unbroken line from roadside to conical summit, looking well worthy of its Gaelic name (which it shares with two other Munros and several other Scottish mountains).

It is the highest mountain not only in the Crianlarich Group but in the whole of Britain south of Ben Lawers (Route 15), with a summit view that is reputed to include half of Scotland. Despite its height and steepness, and despite the encircling forest, Benmore Glen to its west offers an easy ascent route to the 862m/2828ft Bealach-eadar-dha Beinn (*Byalach-aitar-gha Ben*, literally the Bealach-between-two-mountains). This is the aptly named, 300m/1000ft-deep bealach that separates Ben More and Stob Binnein and from which each peak can be climbed in turn.

Ston Binnein is a worthy peak in its own right, with a superb ascent route along its south ridge from the end of the minor road through Balquhidder. Given sufficient fitness, however, you'll find its ascent from the bealach an easy add-on to that of Ben More.

Ben More from Benmore Farm via Benmore Glen
NN 414258, 6ml/10km, 1000m/3300ft

BEN MORE

Benmore Glen

Glen Dochart

The route begins at Benmore farm on the A85 2ml/3km east of Crianlarich. From roadside parking just east of the farm, a sign-posted path joins a Land Rover track up Benmore Glen beneath Ben More's grassy western slopes. When the track ends, a somewhat boggy path continues up beside the Benmore Burn.

Your first goal is the Bealach-eadar-dha Beinn. It is tempting to take a diagonal short cut up the grassy hillside to reach the bealach but, if you yield to temptation, you'll find yourself on increasingly steep, pathless terrain. The best line holds to the glen as far as the stream prior to the one that comes down from the bealach. There's a large boulder just before this stream joins the Benmore Burn at NN 421235. A developing path goes up the stream's right-hand side, crosses to the bealach stream and climbs the right-hand side of that past numerous small waterfalls and pools that tempt on a hot day.

Once on the bealach, Ben More's broad south ridge rears overhead, giving a steep but easy 312m/1024ft climb to the ▲summit. A few rock obstacles on the gentle summit slopes are easily bypassed, while some may have more fun going over them.

BEN MORE   STOB BINNEIN

S Ridge

Benmore Glen   Bealach-eadar-dha Beinn

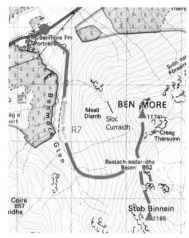

Bonus Munro: Stob Binnein add-on 1ml/1½km, 300m/1000ft

After returning to the bealach, the 303m/994ft return trip up and down Stob Binnein's stony north ridge, rimming broken crags at the head of

Coire Chaorach to the left, is less steep. The zigzagging path soon deposits you on the appealingly castellated ▲summit.

▲**Ben Vorlich** 165 985m/3232ft (OS 57, NN 629189)
For meaning, see Route 3 namesake on Page 10

BEN VORLICH   STUC A' CHROIN

Loch Voil

East of the Crianlarich Group the high country around Loch Earn contains several Corbetts but few Munros. The area is situated on the edge of the Highland Boundary Fault and is characterised by mainly featureless hills, but neighbouring Munros Ben Vorlich and Stuc a' Chroin are picturesque exceptions.

As befits the nearest Munros to Edinburgh, they are popular mountains whose many and varied ascent routes provide a worthy introduction to Southern Highland hillwalking.

When viewed from across Loch Earn, Ben Vorlich's convex upper slopes give it the appearance of a great pudding, but in reality it is an X-shaped mountain whose sky-high twin tops throw out two northern and two southern ridges. The traditional ascent route from Ardvorlich House on Lochearnside to the north has been furnished with a refurbished path that now makes the ascent easy.

Stuc a' Chroin is a more difficult mountain that is most easily reached from the south (Route 10).

Ben Vorlich from Ardvorlich (Loch Earn)
NN 633233, 6ml/10km, 890m/2900ft

This time-honoured ascent route was, until recently, beginning to show its age, becoming literally bogged down, but path renovation has revitalised it and reinstated it as the premier route up Ben Vorlich.

BEN VORLICH

Ardvorlich

Loch Earn

From Ardvorlich House east gate on the South Lochearnside road, follow the driveway up to the buildings, cross a bridge and take the Land Rover track that runs up Glen Vorlich on the right-hand side of the river. About ¾ml/1km beyond the house, just beyond a small stream at NN 630218, a grassy track forks left to continue up the glen. Ignore this track and keep to the main track, which makes a beeline for the summit of Ben Vorlich ahead.

BEN VORLICH

Making a beeline for the summit

The main track ends at the stream coming down from the great scallop of Coire Buidhe (*Corra Boo-ya*, Yellow Corrie) on the right. Beyond here an excellently renovated baggers' path makes a rising traverse up the left-hand side of the corrie to top out on Ben Vorlich's north-east ridge at around the 650m/2150ft mark.

BEN VORLICH

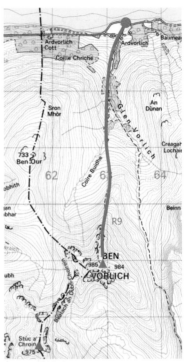

Just before the path turns left for its final climb onto the ridge, note the branch path that continues straight on up the corrie. This is the return route for scramblers who go on to climb Stuc a' Chroin as well.

At the time of writing, renovation ends at the path junction, leaving a short rough section up to the ridge as evidence of the main path's former state. A stony path continues up the ridge between Coire Buidhe to the right and a smaller north-east corrie to the left. The angle is steep for a while, then it eases before steepening again to the summit.

Loch Earn

Coire Buidhe

NE Corrie

BEN VORLICH

The aerial motorway, looking
west along the summit ridge

BEN VORLICH Summit

The tops at each end of the short summit ridge are connected by 100m of path so well-beaten that it amounts to the Highlands' first aerial motorway. The west top and ▲summit, reached first, is 1m/3ft higher than the east top further along.

From the summit the whole ascent route is laid out below, leading the eye north over Loch Earn to the Lawers Range. But it is the newly revealed view of the Prow of Stuc a' Chroin to the south that will rivet the attention (picture on Page 40).

Looking east along the
summit ridge in winter

BEN VORLICH E top

▲Stuc a' Chroin 182 975m/3199ft (OS 57, NN 617174)
Stoochk a Chroa-in, probably Peak of the Sheepfold

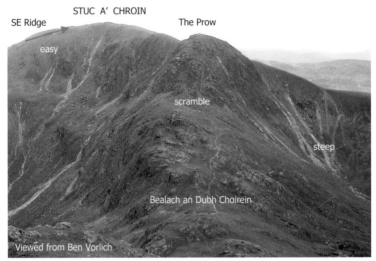

STUC A' CHROIN

SE Ridge

The Prow

easy

scramble

steep

Bealach an Dubh Choirein

Viewed from Ben Vorlich

S tuc a' Chroin is a more retiring mountain than its neighbour Ben Vorlich, from which it is separated by the deep Bealach an Dubh Choirein (*Byalach an Doo Chorrin*, Pass of the Black Corries). The two Munros are often climbed together, but anyone approaching from Ben Vorlich must be prepared to take on The Prow, one of the Southern Highlands' most outstanding mountain features.

The crest of The Prow is a hard scramble, while an exposed, gritty path right of the crest avoids the most difficult sections. There's also a bypass path up the little corrie further right, but this too is too steep and rough for anyone seeking an easy route to Stuc

a' Chroin's summit.

Another approach, from the A84 north of Callander, begins beside Loch Lubnaig to the west. This offers a non-scrambling ascent that is the shortest route to the summit, but it crosses steep and complex terrain where good routefinding skills are required.

The easiest ascent route, described here, begins nearer Callander and approaches the summit via the south-east ridge. This long, lonely, languid ridge of beautiful grass lies in remote country far from main roads. Although not the most heavily trodden route up Stuc a' Chroin, it gives an easy and rewarding ascent that feels both wild and tame at the same time.

Stuc a' Chroin from the South-east (Callander)
NN 636107, 12ml/19km, 810m/2650ft

The route begins at the end of the minor road that leaves the A84 in Callander to run north past Bracklinn Falls. There are parking spaces at the end of the public road, where a branch forks left to the farm at Drumardoch. Follow the continuing Land Rover track past Braeleny farm to the boarded-up buildings at Arivurichardich (try saying that fast).

STUC A' CHROIN   SE Ridge   Meall na h-Iolaire

From Callander

Just before Arivurichardich the track crosses the Keltie Water, whose bridge was washed away by storms in 2004. On a good day you can use stepping stones to cross both the river and a tributary just upstream of the former bridge. At other times you may need to paddle. And remember there are yet other times when the water is high enough to wash away a bridge.

STUC A' CHROIN   The Prow

SE Ridge

From the left-hand side of the upper building at Arivurichardich, the route continues on a former stalkers' path that has seen better days but still gives reasonably good going (except after rain). After a couple of hundred metres, at a fence, it forks. Take the right branch to climb diagonally up the hillside onto the south-east ridge of Stuc a' Chroin, reaching the skyline near the small hump of Meall na h-Iolaire (*Myowl na Hillyera*, Hill of the Eagle).

A baggers' path continues up the broad ridge, which revels in the quixotic name of Aonach Gaineamhach (*Ernach Ganavach*, Ridge of Fine Sand). After surmounting Meall na h-Iolaire the angle eases and, on excellent grassy terrain,

the ridge rises pleasantly to a final steepening and Stuc a' Chroin's flat ▲summit. You'll want to pause awhile here to take in the northern view of Ben Vorlich, and you may well decide to stroll a further 500m along a broad stretch of ridge for

a view over the top of the Prow.

On descent the south-east ridge gives a perfect evening stravaig down the beguiling greensward before the path heads glenwards to rejoin the approach track at Arivurichardich.

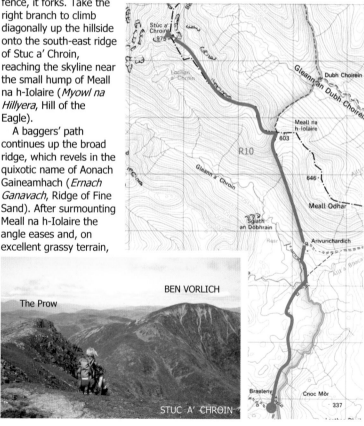

The Prow

BEN VORLICH

STUC A' CHROIN

▲Ben Chonzie 250 931m/3054ft (OS 51 or 52, NN 773308)
Ben Honzie, probably Mossy Mountain (from Gaelic *choinnich*), also known as Ben-y-Hone

S ituated on the edge of the Highlands north-east of Loch Earn, lumpen Ben Chonzie is generally regarded as being one of the dullest of all Munros. With its phenomenally phlat summit, physically pheatureless phlanks and equally phorm-phree surrounding hills, it wouldn't merit a second glance had it not managed to heave itself up over the 3000ft mark.

Nevertheless, the ease of the ascent prompts us to suggest (in a whisper, and please don't tell anyone we said so) that the summit makes a more than amiable objective for some elevation gain on a phine day.

A south-west approach from Glen Lednock is 1ml/2km shorter than a south-east approach from Loch Turret and has a good track that climbs high up the mountain. However, we prefer the Loch Turret approach, which is more scenic, has 150m/500ft less ascent and allows for a round trip.

The route is on both OS 51 & OS 52 but, if using OS 51, the start is just off it.

Ben Chonzie from Loch Turret
NN 822266, 10ml/16km, 570m/1850ft

The south-eastern approach to Ben Chonzie is made scenic by a glacial trench that contains two bodies of water: a large reservoir (Loch Turret) and a small lochan (Lochan Uaine, *Lochan Oo-anya*, Green Lochan). Note that the road to Loch Turret dam north of Crieff is open to the public despite any notices you may see to the contrary.

notch

Carn Chois

Loch Turret

Drumlins

Lochan Uaine

The approach route viewed from the notch

Drumlins (from the Gaelic *druim*, meaning ridge) are small hillocks formed beneath a glacier as it moves over uneven ground, depositing rocks and sediment as it progresses. They often occur in clusters and are elongated in the direction of flow, with a steep slope facing uphill and a lee slope facing downhill.

From the dam car park, a vehicle track along the east side of the loch runs all the way to Lochan Uaine at the foot of the mountain's upper slopes, 440m/1450ft below the summit. The picturesque lochside stroll takes you through the ice-scoured trench and past an attractive clutch of heather-clad drumlins at Loch Turret's head. Beyond here, the track is less well-surfaced but continues to give good going to its end at Lochan Uaine.

When the track ends the climb proper begins. Keep going in the same north-westerly direction to follow traces of path up the hillside, eventually to climb a rake of grass and boulders that tops out at an obvious notch on the skyline. The going is rough for a while but the ascent remains straightforward.

Once up, turn left to follow an old fence up easy convex slopes to Chonzie's grassy ▲summit dome (not a place to linger if the cloud descends).

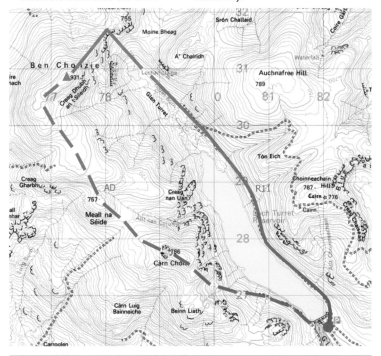

After a phun-philled phootslog, make sure you're down in time for afternoon tea at Glenturret Distillery, passed on the road to Loch Turret.

Alternative Descent: High-level Return Route
extra mileage: none; extra ascent: 90m/300ft

Rather than come straight back down the mountain, you could make a round trip by returning along the high ground on the west side of Loch Turret. This gives a high-level plateau walk on mostly excellent terrain and paths (although the going can be boggy after rain).

From Chonzie's summit, follow the fence south-west then south-east across the plateau-like ridge to Meall na Seide (*Myowl na Say-ja*, Hill of the Bed of Hay) and Carn Chois (*Carn Choas*, Cairn of the Cave or Crevice). From here, take a diagonal line down the hillside to reach the vehicle track along Loch Turret's west shore.

Gaelic dictionaries give *Seide* in Meall na Seide an alternative meaning: 'a swelling in a person from luxurious living and deep potations.' Of course, an upstanding reader such as your good self will never suffer from such an affliction.

▲Ben Challum 106 1025m/3363ft (OS 50, NN 386322)
Calum's Mountain, possibly named for St. Columba

BEINN DUBHCHRAIG | BEN LUI | S Top | Summit | Ben Challum from the north-east

easy route

North Face

At the head of Glen Lochay, well beyond the road end, Ben Challum's summit tops a craggy north face whose bounding ridges provide adventurous ascent routes for off-the-beaten-path explorers. Another high-level ridge, slung between summit and South Top, gives easier walking in a terrific situation between deep glens to east and west. The good news is that the South Top is easily reached by a much shorter approach from the A82 Tyndrum road on the south side of the mountain.

It has to be said that that, viewed from the roadside, the lower reaches of the sprawling hillside up which the southern route climbs look tiresomely dreary. However, the route improves greatly with height and, from the South Top onwards, you'll be more than glad you made the ascent.

Ben Challum from the south-west | Summit | S Top

Gleann a' Chlachain

Ben Challum from Kirkton Farm (near Tyndrum)
NN 355282, 7ml/11km, 900m/2950ft

From the lay-by on the A82 opposite Kirkton farm, 2ml/3km east of Tyndrum, take the farm access road across the River Fillan (bridge) to join the West Highland Way. Follow the Way to the farm buildings and the ruins of St. Fillan's priory.

Immediately beyond the ruins, when the Way turns left, keep straight on along another farm track that leads up to and across the West Highland Railway line.

BEN CHALLUM   S Top

Creag Loisgte

Dalrigh   Auchtertyre

S Top

Creag Loisgte

About 50m beyond the railway crossing, quit the track to climb diagonally right to a deer fence that can be seen above. Beside the fence you'll find a path that goes all the way to the summit. The fence veers much further right than seems warrantable, but the path hasn't developed here for no reason. Stick with it.

The main interest on this part of the ascent lies in avoiding the numerous sections of marshy ground. About half-way up, when the path temporarily levels off atop Creag Loisgte (*Craik Loshka*, possibly Burning Crag, from Gaelic *Loisg*), there's one stretch of bog that is particularly amusing.

St. Columba was an Irish monk who brought Christianity to Scotland in 563. St. Fillan was a later Irish monk who came to what is now Strath Fillan in the seventh or eight century and established a monastery at or near Kirkton farm. For centuries the sanctuary was a haven of peace and learning in troubled times. In the fourteenth century Robert Bruce upgraded it to a priory, which it remained until falling into disrepair after the Reformation of the seventeenth century.

Beyond Creag Loisgte, with the skyline of the South Top in view at last, the path continues its ascent on the right of the now broken fence. The angle steepens but improved going more than compensates, courtesy of a stony path that climbs slopes of short grass and boulders.

Matters become more interesting at the ΔSouth Top, where a curious little defile separates the cairned highpoint from the continuing ridge to Ben Challum's summit. For a short stretch

Creag Loisgte

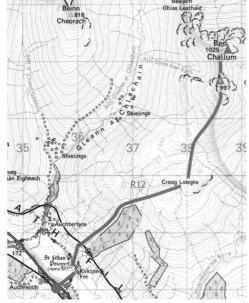

A Land Rover track, part of the West Highland Way, connects Kirkton farm to Auchtertyre farm about ½ml/1km away. Here you'll find all kinds of accommodation (rooms, wigwams, camping) plus an all-year-round shop/café that makes a great little whistle-stop at the end of the day.

You could even use it as an alternative starting point for the route (NN 354290). The access road to the car park leaves the A82 at NN 349288.

If it's okay with you, and even if it isn't, I'll sit on a bench in the sun and sip tea while you nip up Ben Challum.
Address: Auchtertyre Farm, Tyndrum, Perthshire FK20 8RU. Tel: 01838-400251.

Looking north along the summit ridge from the S Top

Summit

the ridge is quite narrow and rocky, though of zero difficulty and of such interest that one wishes it continued further in this vein.

It soon becomes grassy again as it crosses a shallow bealach to reach steeper, rockier slopes that climb to the ▲summit. Broad enough to be easy yet narrow enough to afford views down each side, it gives the kind of sky-high ridge walk for which the Scottish Highlands were designed.

S Top

Looking south along the summit ridge from the summit

▲Meall Glas 199 959m/3146ft (OS 51, NN 431321)
Myowl Glass, Green-grey Hill

Beinn Cheathaich

MEALL GLAS

Glen Lochay

At the west end of Loch Tay, Glen Lochay curves deep into the hills north of the Tyndrum/Crianlarich/Killin road through Strath Fillan and Glen Dochart to give access to a number of flanking Munros. While the glen itself is picturesque enough, in a green, serene and undemanding kind of way, the featureless hillsides that rise to the heights are rather less inspiring. The summits themselves are nevertheless scenic objectives. This guidebook includes two routes that give easy approaches across otherwise boggy and frustrating terrain.

The summits of neighbours Meall Glas and Sgiath Chuil (*Skee-a Choo-il,* Back Wing) recede above sprawling moor and barely rate a second glance when viewed from the main road. Older guidebooks suggest an approach from this side but from Glen Lochay to the north the summits look much more attractive. More importantly, access to Meall Glas from this side has been revolutionised in recent years by a Land Rover track that climbs to within 300m/1000ft of the summit plateau.

Meall Glas from Kenknock (Glen Lochay)
NN 466364, 10ml/16km, 890m/2900ft

Fording the River Lochay

From the car park at the end of the public road up Glen Lyon, just beyond Kenknock farm, take the continuing Land Rover track beside the River Lochay and fork left at a junction after c.1ml/1½km. The left branch fords the river and so must you, as the bridge marked on older maps at NN 453356 no longer exists. The crossing is normally an easy paddle (but one that must be repeated on the return trip).

Across the river, the track passes the old boarded-up building at Lubchurran and climbs the glen behind it towards the Lairig a' Churain (*Lahrik a Chooran*, Carrot Pass) between Sgiath Chuil and Meall Glas. Before reaching the lairig, the track abandons the glen to curve right onto the broad north ridge of Beinn Cheathaich (Ben *Chay-ich*, Misty Mountain), the Top at the north end of Meall Glas's mile-long summit plateau.

Meall a' Churain   SGIATH CHUIL
The track to Beinn Cheathaich

Beinn Cheathaich

End of track
Viewed from Meall a' Churain

The track ends on boggy flats at a height of 670m/2200ft, from where easy slopes of grass then heath continue to ΔBeinn Cheathaich.

N.B. At the point where the track bears right towards the north ridge it is tempting to abandon it for a more direct route to the summit, but you'll find much gentler and easier going on the ridge itself. As you ascend, note the horribly steep slopes that climb to Sgiath Chuil across the boggy Lairig a' Churain to the left.

Once up Beinn Cheathaich, a broad, grassy ridge-cum-plateau curves over the rounded

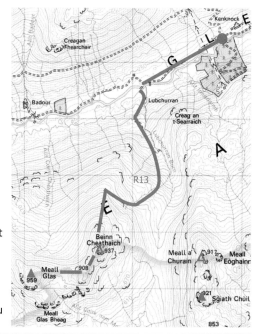

Meall Glas Beag

MEALL GLAS

Beinn Cheathaich

Beinn Cheathaich — Meall a' Churain — SGIATH CHUIL — Meall Glas Beag — MEALL GLAS

rise of Meall Glas Beag (*Bake*, Little; Point 908 on OS map) to the dome-like ▲summit of Meall Glas. A good path takes the line of least resistance by skirting Meall Glas Beag. After taking

in the excellent all-round summit view, retrace your steps to Beinn Cheathaich and re-descend the approach track, all the while looking forward to another bracing ford of the River Lochay.

Meall a' Churain — SGIATH CHUIL — Lairig a' Churain — Beinn Cheathaich

Viewed from Beinn Cheathaich, Sgiath Chuil looks temptingly close at hand, but it lies on the far side of the deep, peaty pass of the Lairig a' Churain. A safe crossing from one Munro to the other involves negotiating intimidatingly steep hillsides that rise over 300m/1000ft on each side of the pass, to say nothing of peat hags and tangled heather on the lairig itself.

In the original 1891 Tables, Meall Glas was a Top and Beinn Cheathaich was the Munro. This unlikely state of affairs came about because only Beinn Cheathaich was named on Munro's map. The position was reversed in 1921. The same happened to Sgiath Chuil (originally a Top) and its Top Meall a' Churain (originally the Munro).

▲**Meall Ghaordaidh** 93 1039m/3409ft (OS 51, NN 514397)
Myowl Geuh-dy, meaning obscure. Traditionally translated as Hill of the Arm or Shoulder (from Gaelic *Gairdean*, the upper part of the arm), but other derivations are possible. *Gaothar* means Windy, and the isolated summit can certainly be that.

MEALL GHAORDAIDH

SE Ridge

Glen Lochay

M eall Ghaordaidh is a big grassy heap to end all big grassy heaps, but compared to some big grassy Glen Lochay heaps it is a geomorphological masterpiece whose southern slopes rise in an unbroken sweep from glen to summit.

When viewed from Glen Lyon to the north, the mountain initially seems more interesting, with three ridges that end abruptly at rocky bluffs overlooking the glen, like a poor man's Three Sisters of Glen Coe.

However, a long drive into upper Glen Lyon, to trudge up either of the two untracked corries between the bluffs, will in practice prove no more spiritually enlightening than the Glen Lochay approach.

From Glen Lochay that unbroken sweep of uniform hillside that climbs to the summit promises either a monotonous plod or a pleasant afternoon stroll, according to inclination. Whichever you expect, it delivers.

Tip: Unless you enjoy wading through the squelchy stuff, leave the ascent for a day when the ground is fairly dry.

Meall Ghaordaidh from Glen Lochay
NN 527363, 5ml/8km, 890m/2900ft

This route is a plodmeister's dream – straight up and straight back down again. You can begin anywhere at the mountain's foot, but the easiest approach begins on the west side of the bridge over the Allt Dhuin Croisg, just beyond Duncroisk house. Above here, an ill-defined south-east ridge gives the best going and the gentlest angle of ascent.

Begin 50m beyond the bridge (parking at a lay-by 100m further along), where a gate gives access to a farm track. Follow the track through grassy fields and up beside the Allt Dhuin Croisg, whose waters are now captured higher up by the area's hydro-electric scheme.

The track becomes indistinct on grass but remains easy enough to follow to a stile over a dry-stone wall. You could bear left here and make a bee-line for Ghaordaidh's summit, but you wouldn't appreciate the acres of bracken you'd have to wade through. Instead, keep to the now distinct track that continues straight on up the hillside, parallel to the stream, heading for the foot of the south-east ridge.

Leave the track at a brief levelling where some wooden sleepers have been laid over a boggy section, waymarked by a metal pole above left. An ATV track climbs diagonally left to become a path up the ridge. To begin with, it is indistinct and hard to follow in places. If you haven't found it by the time you reach a fence that crosses the hillside, seek it out beside the fence. The terrain above becomes rougher and more tussocky, such that the path increasingly makes a real difference to the pleasantness of the ascent.

In actuality, the path above the fence divides into two virtually parallel paths. The main path climbs the left side of the broad crest of the ridge

MEALL GHAORDAIDH   SE Ridge

Glen Lochay

and is considerably boggy after rain. The other, smaller path climbs further right and is less boggy. You probably won't have a choice of route because the fork occurs (and is probably caused by) indistinct ground. Whichever path you end up on, it is probably best to stick to it.

The summit stays resolutely out of sight as you tramp up the convex hill-side, with nothing to occupy the mind except to wonder if the summit ever *will* come into view. Couple this with an easy-angled slope and there's a tendency to push too hard. Result: knackeredness. Of course, the ridge *does* eventually level off, but only in order to deposit you in a morass of peat hags at the foot of steeper final slopes. The better of the two paths now runs left of the peat, on the ridge crest. The path to the right of the peat is better to begin with but soon contours away from the summit and becomes indistinct; if you're on it, cross to the path on the left.

Although it doesn't seem possible, the summit is still c.300m/1000ft above, such that the final slopes go on

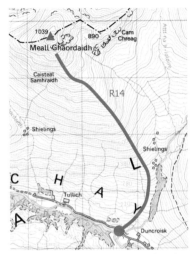

longer than expected. At least there's some definition to the landscape at last, courtesy of small rock outcrops that break out of the hillside. The path climbs left of the largest outcrops, where a stiff pull brings you to the small table-top ▲summit with its large windbreak and excellent all-round views. The windbreak is not large for no reason.

MEALL GHAORDAIDH

▲**Ben Lawers** 10 1214m/3983ft (OS 51, NN 636414)
Hoof-shaped Mountain (from Gaelic *Ladhar*, perhaps referring to the
shape of the eastern corrie skyline) or possibly Loud Mountain (from
Gaelic *Labhar*, after the sound of a stream – the Lawers Burn?)

▲**Beinn Ghlas** 47 1103m/3619ft (OS 51, NN 625404)
Ben Glass, Green-grey Mountain

Telephoto from Kenmore

BEN LAWERS

Loch Tay

I mmediately east of Glen Lochay
(Routes 13 & 14), a group of eight
prominent Munros lords it over the
north shore of Loch Tay. Seven of
them form the Lawers Range, named
for the highest mountain in the
Southern Highlands. Access to the
peaks is facilitated by a minor road
that crosses from Loch Tay to Glen
Lyon, passing between the Lawers
Range and Meall nan Tarmachan (the
eighth Munro, Route 18) and reaching
a high point of 550m/1800ft beside

Lochan na Lairige (*Lochan na Lahrike*,
Lochan of the Pass).

Ease of access is complemented by
a visitor car park, a nature trail and
various renovated paths, making the
area one of the most popular leisure
destinations in the Southern
Highlands, and not just with Munro
baggers. Nowhere more than here
do we hillwalkers have to share our
treasured sanctuary with oxygen-
starved lowlanders spilling shakily out
of their cars to take their first tentative

toddlers' steps in The Great Outdoors.

The mountains are characterised by sweeping green hillsides and high, mostly grassy ridges, along which you can stravaig to your heart's content between picturesque Glen Lyon and the equally picturesque 14½ml/23km ribbon of Loch Tay.

With a vast hillside dropping uniformly to Loch Tay, Ben Lawers gives an impression of great height and makes a fitting highest Southern Highland Munro. It is the highest peak in Britain south of Ben Nevis and, from its summit, we are assured that, on a good day, you can see both the Atlantic to the west and the North Sea to the east.

The mountain lies in the centre of its range, with three Munros to either side of it, yet is far from inaccessible. Thanks to a high starting point on the Lochan na Lairige road, it possesses the peculiar distinction of having the shortest way to its summit cross an intervening Munro – Beinn Ghlas.

The gap between the two requires a descent of only 100m/350ft, which makes Beinn Ghlas very lucky to find itself listed in the Tables as a Munro. Yet it has considerable presence, so we don't begrudge it its status. It towers above the Visitor Centre, from where tourists often mistake it for its hidden neighbour.

Owing to the high starting point, an approach via Beinn Ghlas is understandably the most popular route up Lawers, especially since the refurbishment of the path. Fortunately it is a fine route too, and one on which you get two considerable Munros for the price of one.

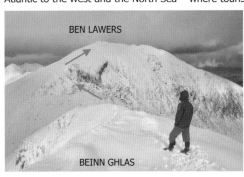

BEN LAWERS

BEINN GHLAS

The Lawers Range was one of the first sites to be purchased by the National Trust for Scotland (NTS) in 1950, largely to ensure the preservation of its unrivalled alpine flora. Six of the seven Munros can be reached from the car park without leaving NTS land, which makes ascents from here the only Munro routes in the Southern Highlands, apart from Route 25 up Schiehallion, that are not subject to stalking considerations.

The range's uniqueness derives from a combination of factors, including climate and altitude, but the main feature that distinguishes it from other Southern Highland upland areas is its geology. Strata of mineral-rich schists break down into soils that are alkaline rather than the more normal acid, enabling plants like alpine saxifrage and alpine lady's mantle to survive.

For more information, before we betray our level of botanical ignorance, visit the website www.nts.org.uk/Property/94.

It goes without saying, but we'll say it anyway: *Do not pick the flowers*.

Ben Lawers (& Beinn Ghlas) from Lawers car park
NN 609379, 6ml/10km, 980m/3200ft

At a starting height of 430m/ 1400ft, and with Loch Tay sparkling in the glen below (there *have* been unsubstantiated reports of sunshine), you are in the presence of handsome high mountain scenery even before you boot up. An excellent renovated path zigzags 670m/2200ft up the south-west ridge of Beinn Ghlas, then a ridge-top path continues to Ben Lawers. It all adds up to a superb leg-stretch.

BEINN GHLAS

Burn of Edramucky

The building at the car park, situated near the high point of the Lochan na Lairige road, is the former Visitor Centre. To reduce costs, the NTS was forced to close it in 2009 after 36 years of operation. It may re-open in the future. Further details at www.nts.org.uk/Property/94.

The Nature Trail still makes a tolerable objective for an afternoon tootle from Killin between admiring the Falls of Dochart and sampling the village's tea rooms. Small parking fee payable at machine.

From the car park the path makes a beeline for Beinn Ghlas, whose domed summit rises ahead atop its gentle south-west ridge. At first the route follows the nature trail on the left of the Burn of Edramucky. When a side path forks left after c.800m, follow the main path across the burn. Ignore a second side path, this time to the right, which takes the nature trail back down to the car park, and continue up to a gate in a fence that gives access to open hillside.

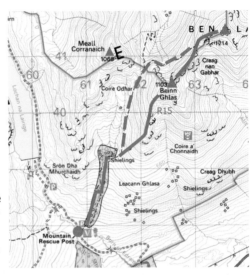

Winter sun highlights the SW Ridge of Beinn Ghlas

Loch Tay

NTS visitor car park

The high starting point makes this a popular winter route but inexperienced walkers often underestimate the dangers. Wind and sun on the south-facing slopes combine to produce freeze/thaw cycles that can result in very icy going. This in turn makes the slopes leading up to the two summits more steep, more exposed and more dangerous than you would imagine from a summer visit. Some attempt the climb without ice axe and crampons but we trust you are not so foolhardy.

Coire Odhar, on the left as you climb Beinn Glas, was at one time a major centre of Scottish skiing. Its gentle, grassy, rock-free slopes require only a modest covering of snow to be in condition.

In the 1950s early ski tows were erected to aid uplift but, as interest in the sport grew, the crowds moved on to the greater snow-holding corries of Glen Coe and the Cairngorms.

A Scottish Ski Club hut was built in the bowl of the corrie in 1932 but had to be demolished in 1999 after it was blown down by a winter storm.

About 150m beyond the fence, the path forks at a conspicuous boulder. The left branch continues up Coire Odhar (*Corra Oa-ar*, Dun-coloured Corrie) to the Meall Corranaich–Beinn Ghlas bealach and is a possible return route. For now, keep right to follow the zigzagging Beinn Ghlas path up the hillside onto the south-west ridge, then onwards and upwards to the abrupt ▲summit overlooking the long northern glen of the Allt a' Chobhair (*Owlt a Ko-ur*, Foaming Stream).

The summit of Ben Lawers, now in view at last, looks distant from here, but appearances are deceptive. With a

Ben Lawers' height and situation (it stands almost in the centre of Scotland) give it tremendous all-round views of the Southern Highlands. Geologist John Macculloch, one of the earliest Highland visitors to find the mountains interesting protuberances rather than useless blots on the landscape, wrote in his 1824 book *The Highlands and Islands of Scotland* that the view from the summit was the best in the country (Ben Lomond came second).

N.B. We believe he might have changed his mind had he climbed Meall Buidhe (Route 23).

BEN LAWERS

AN STUC   MEALL GARBH

BEINN GHLAS

height loss of only 100m/350ft, the path down the connecting ridge to the intervening gap gives a gentle skip-&-saunter that you'll wish was longer. A re-ascent of only 210m/700ft leads more steeply but still easily to Lawers' rocky ▲summit eyrie, perched at the apex of three distinct ridges.

To return, reverse the route. From the bealach between the two Munros, a bypass path contours around the summit of Beinn Ghlas, crosses the bealach to its north-west (below Meall Corranaich) and descends Coire Odhar, eventually to rejoin the ascent path at the conspicuous boulder noted above. This provides variety on the way back, but the path is less well surfaced than the ridge path and views are curtailed. For the small amount of extra effort involved, we'd go back over Beinn Ghlas.

The redoubtable pyramid of An Stuc (*An Stoochk*, The Peak), the next Lawers Range Munro to the east, is an awkward customer to reach from most starting points. Consequently some opt to tackle it via the steep but scramble-free connecting ridge from Ben Lawers. The fitness-testing return trip is 2½ml/4km long and requires 470m/1550ft of ascent.

AN STUC   MEALL GARBH

Creag an Fhithich

Lochan nan Cat

BEN LAWERS

▲**Meall Corranaich** 68 1069m/3507ft (OS 51, NN 615410)
Myowl Corranich, possible meanings include Hill of the Lament (from Gaelic *Corranach*), Hill of the Bracken Corrie (from Gaelic *Coire Raineach*) and Sickle-shaped Hill (from Gaelic *Corran*)
▲**Meall a' Choire Leith** 261 926m/3038ft (OS 51, NN 612439) *Myowl a Chorra Lay*, Hill of the Grey Corrie

Viewed from Meall nan Tarmachan

MEALL CORRANAICH   BEN LAWERS   BEINN GHLAS

Lochan na Lairige

These two rounded summits to the north-west of Beinn Ghlas complete the trio of Munros west of Ben Lawers. Overshadowed in bulk by Lawers to the east and in ruggedness by Meall nan Tarmachan to the west, they are the highpoints on a gentle grassy ridge that runs north-south beside the Lochan na Lairige road.

The most practicable and popular way of bagging the pair begins at the road's highpoint, 3ml/5km north of Lawers visitor car park. From here the two summits are equidistant, making a circular trip possible. Unfortunately, boggy approaches make for a 'mixed' hillwalking experience, definitely not one for which the Lawers Range would prefer to be remembered.

In this guidebook we describe the ascent of Meall Corranaich by its easy south-east ridge and leave the more awkward continuation to Meall a' Chore Leith for those who enjoy heading off-path down steep hillsides and revelling in the squelchy stuff.

Meall Corranaich from Lochan na Lairige road highpoint
NN 593416, 4ml/7km, 520m/1700ft

From the cairn at the highpoint of the Lochan na Lairige road, 3ml/5km beyond Lawers car park, the ridge that curves to the summit of Meall Corranaich makes an obvious approach route. From the parking space below the cairn, walk back along the road, around the bend, to find the start of the path just before the first passing place. N.B. Don't confuse this path with the return path from Meall a' Choire Leith, which leaves the road 20m earlier, at the corner.

The path is boggy at first as it climbs to the crest of the ridge but it improves higher up. The route follows the boundary line marked on the OS map and which is marked on the ground by a line of old fence posts. There are zero features of interest to

MEALL CORRANAICH

The path leaves the ridge crest to take a short cut

warrant description. Higher up, as the ridge curves from south to east, the path leaves the broad crest to take a short cut across the bend. Eventually it joins the more well-defined south-west ridge for the final part of the ascent to Meall Corranaich's ▲summit.

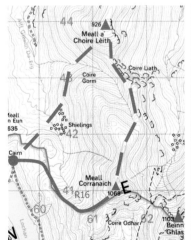

Looking back down the lower ridge

Viewed from Meall a' Choire Leith

MEALL CORRANAICH

Coire Gorm

Bonus Munro: Meall a' Choire Leith add-on 2ml/3km, 210m/700ft

From Meall Corranaich a broad, gentle ridge connects to Meall a' Choire Leith, but read on before you are seduced by it. A good path leads off across short turf then, after a short rise, the ridge broadens even more and divides around Coire Gorm (*Corra Gorram*, Blue Corrie). The lie of the land tempts you left onto the corrie's left-hand rim. Instead, keep right to follow the right-hand rim up to the flat ▲summit of Meall a' Choire Leith.

The problem is: what now? As a return via Meall Corranaich would involve another 300m/1000ft ascent back to its summit, the standard return route takes a more direct line down to the roadside. Descend Meall a' Choire Leith's steep, grassy south-west slopes into Coire Gorm and tramp up the boggy upper reaches of Gleann Da-Eig. A swampy path takes the best line, crossing the Allt Gleann Da-Eig at a small dam, but in many places it is more of a hindrance than a help.

Cross the low bealach south of the hillock called Meall nan Eun (*Myowl nan Ee-an*, Hill of the Birds) to regain the roadside. As a parting shot by which to remember the two Munros, the peat hags on the bealach will act as a litmus test of your capacity to maintain a humorous disposition in the most dire of circumstances.

MEALL A' CHOIRE LEITH

Viewed from Meall Corranaich

▲**Meall Greigh** 136 1001m/3284ft (OS 51, NN 674438) *Myowl Gray*, usually translated as Hill of the Herd (of Cattle or Horses). Another beautiful meaning of the Gaelic word *Greigh*, despite its English pronunciation, is: 'uncommon heat of the sun after bursting out from under a cloud.' On the other hand, older maps (including the one that Sir Hugh used) named the mountain Meall Gruaidh (*Myowl Groo-y*), meaning Hill of the Profile or Cheek.

▲**Meall Garbh** 35 1118m/3668ft (OS 51, NN 644436) *Myowl Garrav*, Rough Hill

BEN LAWERS

MEALL GREIGH

Loch Tay

Viewed from Kenmore

Ben Lawers and the three Munros to its east form the skyline of the Lawers Range's finest feature – the great eastern corrie. Its deepest recesses, hard under the crags of An Stuc, shelter shapely Lochan nan Cat, whose very existence remains unknown to the vast majority of visitors who motor over the Lochan na Lairige road further west.

Tumbling down the corrie into Loch Tay is the Lawers Burn, whose banks carry a path that gives one of the best approach walks in the Southern

Highlands. Once up, the round of the corrie skyline, beginning on Meall Greigh and crossing Meall Garbh and An Stuc to Ben Lawers, is the range's most scenic and exciting route.

As you climb beside the Lawers Burn, Meall Greigh is the first Munro on the right (east) and its grassy summit is easily reached. Meall Garbh, the next Munro along, is equally easy to reach, such that the pair are often climbed together. Further along the skyline, An Stuc and Ben Lawers are more serious propositions.

Meall Greigh from Lawers Village (Loch Tay)
NN 680400, 7ml/11km, 820m/2700ft

The route begins on the A827 Loch Tay road, at the foot of the Lawers Burn in Lawers village, beside a horn carver's showroom. Parking is notoriously restricted. At the time of writing, it is possible to park at the horn carver's car park for a fee, or at the Lawers Hotel, further along the road towards Killin, if you purchase refreshment on return.

MEALL GARBH   MEALL GREIGH

Loch Tay

MEALL GREIGH   Sron Mhor

The Lawers Burn path

Begin on the access track that climbs behind the showroom to Machuim Farm. Follow signs around the farm buildings and you'll soon reach the beautifully constructed path that climbs into Ben Lawers' eastern corrie beside the deep-cut Lawers Burn. The path crosses the burn at a bridge (NN 673420) and climbs to a

Land Rover track, which continues to a small dam in the bowl of the corrie (NN 662427).

From here, easy slopes climb to the Meall Greigh – Meall Garbh bealach, from which each Munro can be climbed in turn. However, it is normal to leave the path before its end to take a more direct line up Meall Greigh's grassy hillside.

MEALL GREIGH

Descent route

Route to Meall Garbh

The most scenic route up, giving views along the length of Loch Tay, goes straight up the south-east ridge over the unfortunately named Sron Mhor (*Strawn Voar*, Big Nose). For gentler grass slopes, keep to the path as far as the bridge, then continue along the near side of the burn on a

good sheep path that will be found a few metres up the slope on the right.

When you reach the first appreciable stream coming down from Meall Greigh, climb its left-hand side. Higher up, trend right onto the skyline to find a path leading to the pudding-shaped ▲summit.

For a gentler descent, return via the bealach below Meall Garbh. The path down to the bealach is boggy and indistinct in places but the route is obvious in fine weather and easy grass slopes descend from the bealach to the dam on the Lawers Burn.

Below here, follow a Land Rover track for c.300m, then branch left on the Lawers Burn path (cairn) for a glorious walk down to your starting point. Some 800m down, keep a lookout for a fork where the main path appears to go straight on but in fact zigzags down left to the bridge noted above.

The Lawers Burn cuts a curiously deep trench into the hillside, with raised banks that are additionally notable for their innumerable ruined dwellings, especially at East Mealour (NN 676415). These are a poignant reminder of the days when Lawers village was the populous centre of a flax spinning industry.

Once you've reached the Lawers Burn dam you may wish to visit the shores of Lochan nan Cat. A path of sorts (boggy after rain) follows the south bank of the burn from the dam to the lochan's mouth (1200m each way).

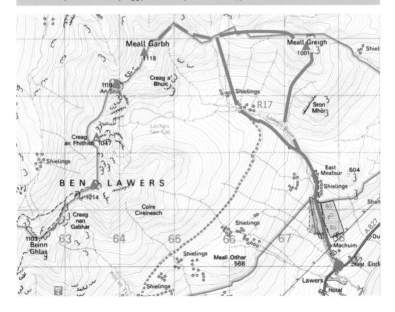

Bonus Munro: Meall Garbh add-on 2ml/3km, 280m/900ft

Meall Garbh is in many ways a more interesting peak than Meall Greigh and is well worth bagging if you have the energy. The 834m/2736ft bealach between the two Munros is known as the Lairig Innein (*Lahrik Inyan*, Anvil Pass, unnamed on OS map). From it, steeper grass slopes climb to Meall Garbh's north-west shoulder, where the angle of ascent eases as the ridge veers south-west around the head of the eastern corrie.

MEALL GARBH

Lairig Innein

Route from Meall Griegh

A couple of hundred metres before the summit, you'll pass a curious transverse ridge, whose cairned high-point can mislead in cloud. At the ▲summit itself, the view west opens up and affords a first opportunity to study in detail the imposing north-east face of An Stuc. One look may be enough to send you scampering back down to the bealach.

BEN LAWERS

AN STUC

MEALL GARBH

Avoid

Lochan nan Cat

Warning: On the map it may seem tempting to descend from Meall Garbh to the An Stuc bealach and from there to the head of Lochan nan Cat beside a tumbling stream, but the hillside below the bealach consists of very steep, wet grass among sizeable crags. Avoid.

BEN
LAWERS

BEINN
GHLAS

AN STUC

N Ridge

NE
Face

Bypass
path

MEALL GARBH

An Stuc is not an easy option from the Meall Garbh side. Since the peak's promotion to Munro status in 1997 the scramble up the north-east face is becoming increasingly eroded to a worrying degree. A small bypass path crosses steep ground to the right, but it is more suitable for sheep than humans and sensitive souls may well find it exposed in places.

Those who make it up continue over Ben Lawers to complete a circuit of the eastern corrie skyline.

▲Meall nan Tarmachan 89 1044m/3425ft (OS 51, NN 585390) *Myowl nan Tarmachan*, Ptarmigan Hill

Creag na Caillich | Beinn nan Eachan | Meall Garbh | MEALL NAN TARMACHAN | SE Top

Falls of Dochart, Killin

The lone Munro of Meall nan Tarmachan on the west side of the Lochan na Lairige road is somewhat outnumbered by the seven Munros of the Lawers Range on the east side. Yet it does more than hold its own. With four times as many Tops as its neighbour, it forms a miniature mountain range whose twisting skyline (the Tarmachan Ridge) provides a dramatic backdrop to the Falls of Dochart at Killin.

The ridge snakes and undulates along the skyline for 2ml/3km, giving the most exciting ridge walk not only on Loch Tayside but also arguably in the whole Southern Highlands. Sometimes broad, sometimes narrow,

sometimes rocky, sometimes grassy... one characteristic it never lacks is interest. An added attraction is that, from the high starting point of the Lochan na Lairige road, it doesn't take too long to reach the ridge crest.

If that's good news for scramblers, the even better news for those who consider the excitements of exposed ridge walking a mixed pleasure, is that the summit of Meall nan Tarmachan itself is at the near end of the ridge and is easily reached by a renovated path that begins near Lawers car park. What's more, from there you can go for a scenic stroll along the easy first section of the ridge to the next Top (Meall Garbh).

Meall nan Tarmachan from near Lawers car park
NN 605383, 4½ml/ 7km, 650m/2150ft

Begin on the Land Rover track that leaves the Lochan na Lairige road 400m north of Lawers car park. Park with consideration at the start of the track (NN 605383) or at the car park (NN 609379). The track leads to a disused quarry and forms the return route from Creag na Caillich, the fourth and final Top at the far end of the Tarmachan Ridge, for those completing the whole ridge walk.

For the easy route up Meall nan Tarmachan at the near end of the ridge, leave the track at the first

Looking back down the ascent route from near the summit of Meall nan Tarmachan

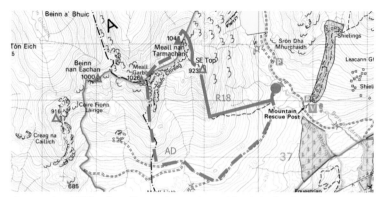

stream, about 500m from the road-side, just over the first rise. Look for a cairn that marks the start of the path up the mountain's grassy south-east shoulder. The path has been excellently renovated and climbs without incident directly to the lowly ΔSouth-east Top.

Over the South-east Top, a short descent leads to the foot of Tarmachan's south-east face and the steepest part of the route. The path climbs a grassy groove on stone steps, then avoids craggier ground above by veering right up a broad, grassy shelf. This leads beneath the summit to reach the skyline on the north-east ridge, close to the ▲summit.

MEALL NAN TARMACHAN

SE Top

Bonus Top: Meall Garbh add-on 1½ml/3km, 80m/250ft

From Meall nan Tarmachan, the Tarmachan Ridge snakes westwards over three lower Tops: ΔMeall Garbh (*Myowl Garrav*, Rough Hill), ΔBeinn nan Eachan (*Ben nan Yechan*, Horse Mountain) and ΔCreag na Caillich (*Craik na Kyle-yich*, Old Woman's Crag)

Meall Garbh, the first Top along, is the most interesting of the lot and can be reached without difficulty by a scenic stroll along the first section of the ridge. We recommend you go take a look.

Meall Garbh

Beinn nan Eachan

MEALL NAN TARMACHAN

The broad ridge leading to Meall Garbh is entertainingly complex, drops only 90m/300ft and harbours two fine lochans. The castellated summit rears up impressively to form an airy knob of rock but the path surmounts it without difficulty.

The descent of the far side of the summit block onto an airy arête, heading onwards to Beinn nan Eachan, involves a couple of moves down a rock step and is a different matter entirely. Many will need no encouragement to go no further.

Winter on the arête beyond Meall Garbh

To avoid retracing steps, and a 90m/300ft climb back to Meall nan Tarmachan, you can descend Meall Garbh's south ridge. Just before the summit, a path leads down onto grassy slopes that fan out to give an easy route back down to the approach track.

▲**Beinn Dorain** 64 1076m/3530ft (OS 50, NN 325378)
Ben Doe-rin, Mountain of the Otter (from Gaelic *Dobhran*) or
Streamlets (from Gaelic *Dobhar*, perhaps referring to its fluted flanks)
▲**36 Beinn an Dothaidh** 129 1004m/3294ft (OS 50, NN
331408) *Ben an Daw-y*, Mountain of Scorching

BEINN DORAIN

S Ridge

Auch Gleann

The Bridge of Orchy mountains form a compact group of five Munros and three Tops that rise to the east of that hamlet on the A82 north of Tyndrum. They are characterised by bold mountains that are linked by long ridges and gouged by craggy corries.

Benn Dorain is the most southerly Munro of the group. When approached along the A82 from Tyndrum to Bridge of Orchy, it appears as a giant cone, making it one of the most distinctive mountains in Scotland.

On its north side, however, the mountain takes pity on hillwalkers by extending a gentler, more complex ridge towards a 744m/2441ft bealach. Not surprisingly, it is this ridge that provides the normal approach route.

On the other side of the bealach the neighbouring Munro of Beinn an Dothaidh can be climbed by an equally easy path for great views over the vast expanse of Rannoch Moor.

Beinn Dorain from Bridge of Orchy
NN 300395, 6ml/10km, 950m/3100ft

Above Bridge of Orchy, Beinn Dorain and Beinn an Dothaidh enclose rugged Coire an Dothaidh, whose head forms their intervening bealach. A path climbs to the bealach from Bridge of Orchy railway station. Parking at the station is reserved for train users, so park at the car park beside Bridge of Orchy Hotel on the A82 and walk up the station road opposite. From the station car park, walk through the underpass, cross the West Highland Way and follow the boot-worn highway up the hill.

Now for the bad news: at the time of writing, the path when wet is an abomination on the face of the earth. The first section is a stony mess... and that's the *best* bit. The central section is a series of muddy morasses that are gradually becoming linked into one great Slough of Despond, almost as bad as the one on Beinn Dubhchraig (Route 5).

In olden days, when mountains were routinely denigrated for their lack of agricultural potential, Beinn Dorain was the first in Scotland to be appreciated purely for its beauty. The instigator of this whole new way of looking at mountains was the eighteenth century gamekeeper and bard Duncan Ban MacIntyre, who wrote a famous poem *Moladh Beinn Dobhrain* (In Praise of Beinn Dorain). With sensibilities far ahead of his time, he described the Ben as 'the most beautiful mountain I have seen under the sun'.

There is a memorial cairn to the bard at his birthplace (NN 263414) – a ruined hillside township reached by an 800m walk up a Land Rover track from the car park near the end of the A8005 west of Bridge of Orchy (NN 271418). N.B. There is a larger memorial cairn on Monument Hill (NN 144259), reached by a minor road past Dalmally station off the A85.

The 'path' impersonates a bog in lower Coire an Dothaidh

But wait... you'll look back fondly on this after the path crosses the stream and impersonates a rocky riverbed as it climbs steeply into the shallow basin of upper Coire an Dothaidh. And here's something else to look forward to: it is even more infernal on descent. If ever a case were needed to justify path restoration programmes, this is it. We recommend you go in a dry spell.

Fortunately, matters improve at the bealach. To the south a steady 332m/1090ft climb up Beinn Dorain's north ridge leads to its summit, while to the north a steeper 260m/853ft climb up Beinn an Dothaidh's south ridge leads to *its* summit.

The well-worn, stony Dorain path climbs steeply at first over slabby ground, then it levels off and turns

The 'path' impersonates a rocky riverbed in upper Coire an Dothaidh

In the whole Southern Highlands, Beinn Dubhchraig included, there is no place that could be more fundamentally improved by the installation of an escalator than Coire an Dothaidh. Copies of our petition are available from the Club secretary.

BEINN DORAIN

BEINN AN DOTHAIDH

sharp right across a small plateau with a lochan. Beyond the lochan, the path turns back left to climb an open grass slope that glories under the entirely unwarranted name of Am Fiaclach (*Am Fee-aclach*, The Teeth). At the top of this the path divides.

The right branch is what appears to be a former sheep path whose increasing prominence testifies to the number of walkers who take it by mistake. It is an awkward, vertiginous little path that undulates across steep, rocky ground on Dorain's west face to reach the south ridge just below the summit. It is a variation best left to sheep, guidebook writers and anyone who has not purchased this book.

The main path stays left, climbs through a small outcrop onto the

False summit

Loch Tulla

BEINN DORAIN   Summit

skyline and, on good going, rises gently up a shoulder to a false summit topped by a large cairn. Just below this to the right, atop a rocky bluff, is a second large cairn curiously known as Carn Sasunaich (*Carn Sassanich*, Englishman's Cairn), a rare acknowledgement in Scottish Highland mountain nomenclature of cross-border infiltration.

The true ▲summit, sporting another large cairn, lies a few minutes further away across a dip. Such is the sprawling complexity of Dorain's north ridge that it is really only on this last section, around the rim of craggy Coire Chruitein (*Corra Chrootin*, Corrie of the Hunchback) that there is any sensation of actually being on a ridge.

Beinn Dorain's false summit has fooled many a mist-enshrouded walker over the years, especially before the path became so distinct. How many Munroists believe they've climbed the mountain but haven't? And who was the unknown Sassenach commemorated by his or her cairn?

BEINN DORAIN summit

Coire Chruitein

False summit

Bonus Munro: Beinn an Dothaidh add-on 1½ml/2km, 280m/950ft

If you intend to climb Beinn an Dothaidh as well, recce the ascent route across the Dorain–Dothaidh bealach as you descend Beinn Dorain. There are two choices. A stony path can be seen climbing diagonally right into a shallow corrie, whose grassy slopes lead up to a broad saddle on the tilted summit plateau between the west top and the summit.

Alternatively, a less distinct path goes up the broad south ridge to the west top, on slopes of grass and rocks left of the corrie. You'll get better views from this ridge, as well as on the scenic stroll from the west top to the summit along the rim of the north-east corrie. As you'll probably want to visit both west top and ▲summit, we'd go up one way and down the other.

▲Beinn Achaladair 94 1038m/3405ft (OS 50, NN 344432)

Ben Achallader, Mountain of the Field by the Hard Water
(from Gaelic *Ach-a-ladair*), named after the farm at its foot

Beinn Achaladair is the Bridge of Orchy Munro north of Beinn Dorain and Beinn an Dothaidh. When viewed from the roadside it seems to consist of nothing more appealing than an extensive and featureless scree-encrusted mountain wall. But, as so often in the Southern Highlands, appearances are deceptive, because that uninviting length of wall buttresses an easy ridge that climbs to a panoramic summit.

> The ruined tower at Achallader farm is all that remains of a Campbell castle that was burned down by the MacDonalds in 1689 during one of many clan skirmishes.

Beinn Achaladair from Achallader farm
NN 322443, 1½ml/18km, 10m/4050ft

As described in Route 19, Beinn an Dothaidh and its southern neighbour Beinn Dorain enclose the double corrie of Coire an Dothaidh, which consists of a deep lower basin leading to a shallow upper basin. In

the same manner, Beinn an Dothaidh and its northern neighbour Beinn Achaladair enclose a double corrie in which lower Coire Achaladair rises to the upper bowl of Coire Daingean (*Corra Dinyun*, Firm or Strong Corrie).

BEINN ACHALADAIR
Summit
S Top
BEINN A'
CHREACHAIN
S Ridge

There the similarity ends. Compared to its southern counterpart, Coire Achaladair/Coire Daingean is a more open and friendlier place, with a gentler angle of ascent (see picture on Page 82). From Achallader farm a path follows the right-hand side of the stream all the way to the Dothaidh–

Achaladair bealach at the corrie head, and you'll be relieved to hear that overall it is in a better state than the one in Coire an Dothaidh. From the bealach, the grassy south ridge climbs to Achaladair's South Top and cliff-edge summit, giving a pleasant and scenic ascent.

On the way back down Beinn Achaladair's scenic south ridge

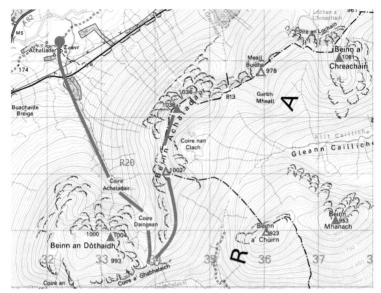

Begin at Achallader farm car park, reached by a dirt road from the A82 on the shores of Loch Tulla. Behind the buildings, a farm track leads to a bridge over the West Highland Railway line, then a path follows a fence to the right-hand bank of the Allt Coire Achaladair and climbs gently into the V-shaped corrie. To keep you on your toes, the path showcases a selection of boggy wallows but, compared to the Coire an Dothaidh path, it's a paragon of virtue. (Even so, we wouldn't go after rain.)

Once it enters Coire Achaladair, the path becomes patience-testingly boggy for a while as it crosses the grassy hillside above the stream, but matters are about to improve so stick with it (sometimes literally). At the head of the corrie the path makes a brief trip across the stream to avoid a crag, then it crosses back and improves immensely as it climbs into the higher Coire Daingean.

BEINN ACHALADAIR

SE Top ←

NE Spur

NE Corrie

Viewed from Meall Buidhe

Even the stream, which up to now has done nothing of note, decides to show off some admirable tumbling skills. After entering the shallow scoop of Coire Daingean, the path meanders pleasantly among grassy knolls and liberal scatterings of bare rock as it makes its final climb to the bealach.

Above the bealach, broad grass slopes rise to Achaladair's ΔSouth Top. A small path soon disappears on boggy ground but reappears higher up when the ridge becomes more well-defined. Over the South Top, a broad saddle leads to Achaladair's long, flat, rocky, confusing summit ridge.

Why confusing? The cairn at the far end, at the edge of a craggy north-east corrie, seems to be the highest point, but the true ▲summit (2m/6ft higher) is a couple of hundred metres before then. Don't miss it, but visit the corrie rim anyway for the expansive view.

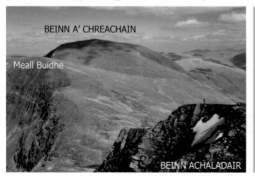

BEINN A' CHREACHAIN

Meall Buidhe

BEINN ACHALADAIR

From Beinn Achaladair it's a long and more difficult walk to Beinn a' Chreachain (*Ben a Chrechin*, Clamshell Mountain), the most northerly Bridge of Orchy Munro. Hands are useful on the initial steep, rocky descent around the rim of Achaladair's NE corrie and there's a long end-of-day walk back from Chreachain via Crannach Wood.

▲**Beinn Mhanach** 211 953m/3127ft (OS 50, NN 373411)
Ben Vanach, Monk Mountain. Contenders include St. Columba (as with nearby Ben Challum), St. Fillan (see Page 49) and Adamnan (Columba's biographer).

Beinn a' Chuirn

BEINN MHANACH

Allt Kinglass

Auch Gleann

This humble, bosomy Munro (it has rounded twin tops) is overshadowed by other Bridge of Orchy mountains in terms of both height and form, and is probably only ever climbed because of its status. It cowers at the head of Auch Gleann behind its four big siblings, but on a hot summer's day you'll find it a pleasant objective in its own right. The reason for this, not apparent from its position on the edge of OS 50, is its isolated situation at the head of Loch Lyon, on OS 51 further east.

Beinn Mhanach and its twin Top Beinn a' Chuirn (*Ben a Hoorn*, Mountain of the Cairn) can be reached from other Bridge of Orchy Munros by convoluted and marshy cross-country routes, but the best approach, in terms of both terrain and scenery, is indisputably along Auch Gleann.

In Sir High's original 1891 Tables, Beinn a' Chuirn was a Munro and Beinn Mhanach was its Top. This erroneous situation was reversed in 1921.

Beinn Mhanach from Auch Farm
NN 317354, 12ml/19km, 890m/2900ft

The approach route to the foot of the mountain follows a 5ml/8km Land Rover track along picturesque Auch Gleann. The twin summits are in view all the way, forming a photogenic composition at the end of the glen. Beinn Mhanach is on the right and Beinn a' Chuirn is on the left.

BEINN DORAIN

Auch Gleann

Waterslides of the Allt a' Chuirn

Begin at the access road to Auch farm on the A82 between Tyndrum and Bridge of Orchy. Park on the road verge, take the paved road down to the farm and follow the continuing Land Rover track along the glen, ignoring all side branches. The track crosses the West Highland Way, fords the Allt Coralan (usually passable dryshod on stepping stones) and passes under the curving viaduct of the West Highland Railway line.

As it progresses up the glen, the track fords the Allt Kinglass four times, giving four easy paddles under normal conditions. Between fords 1 and 2, and again between fords 3 and 4, an occasionally muddy but mostly grassy path runs along the near bank, enabling you to avoid crossing the river at all if you so choose.

When the main river bears left beside some perfectly proportioned drumlins (see Page 44), just before

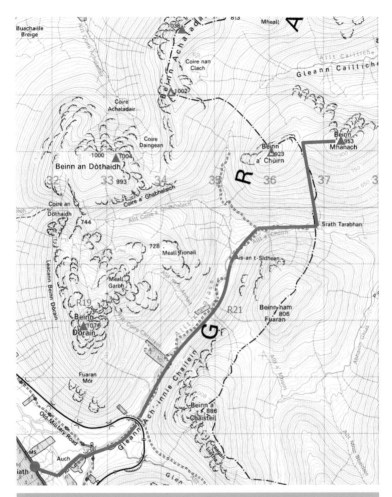

Whereas the right-hand branch of the Auch Gleann track ends at a height of 370m/1200ft on the bealach leading to Loch Lyon, the longer left-hand branch ends at a height of 550m/1800ft beneath the craggy western front of Beinn a'

Chuirn. The additional height makes this a tempting ascent alternative to the one described, but that craggy hillside has to be outflanked on marshy ground further along. Even on descent, to make a round trip, it's not worth the hassle.

the buildings at well-named Ais an t-Sithean (*Ash an Tchee-han*, Back of the Hillocks), the track goes straight on beside a tributary (the Allt a' Chuirn). There are three more fords to come, but by now the stream is usually shallow enough to be crossed on stepping stones.

The track forks at the foot of Beinn a' Chuirn. Follow the right-hand branch to its end on the bealach leading to Loch Lyon, where weirs and waterslides on the Allt a' Chuirn may prove irresistible on a hot day. As an excuse for a lengthy sojourn, you can use the time to study the unfamiliar back sides of Beinn Dorain and Beinn an Dothaidh before tackling the toughest part of the day – a 480m/1550ft ascent on steep grass up Coire a' Chuirn (unnamed on OS map) to the Mhanach–Chuirn saddle above.

The Allt a' Chuirn comes down from the saddle and indicates the line to be taken. The hillside can be climbed on either side of it. On the right-hand side, you can veer away to head directly for Mhanach's summit. More congenially, stay on the left-hand side, where a very rough track gives you a head start, the cooling stream stays close at hand on a hot day, and the angle eases off towards the saddle. Above the saddle, gentle turf slopes climb to the flat, stony ▲summit.

Before descending, you may wish to make the short trip across the intervening saddle to bag ∆Beinn a' Chuirn and obtain a close-up view of the four higher Bridge of Orchy Munros. Reaching the summit requires an ascent of only 74m/243ft.

LAWERS RANGE

Loch Lyon

The view east from Beinn Mhanach

Ais an t-Sithean was once the home of Duncan Ban MacIntyre, Beinn Dorain's poetic champion (see Page 78). There's nothing here now except cowsheds and sheep fanks.

▲**Meall nan Aighean** 169 981m/3218ft (OS 51, NN 694496)
Myowl nan Yun. Aigean means Abyss in Gaelic, but the most likely meaning is Hill of the Fawns or Heifers, from the Gaelic *Agh.*
▲**Carn Mairg** 91 1041m/3415ft (OS 51, NN 684512)
Carn Merrak, Rusty Cairn, from the Gaelic *Meirg,* perhaps referring to autumn colours.

CARN MAIRG

MEALL NAN AIGHEAN

Glen Lyon

Glen Lyon is the longest and arguably the most scenic glen in the Southern Highlands. Sandwiched between the grassy hillsides of the Lawers Range and the Glen Lyon Horseshoe, it eschews dramatic mountainscapes for a serene, sylvan, soothing beauty.

At its heart four Munros link arms to form the crescent-shaped Glen Lyon Horseshoe around the hamlet of Invervar. They are rounded, grassy mountains whose summits are little more than mammary highpoints on a broad, sweeping ridge. That may not sound very appetising, but if the sky is blue and you have a desperate need

to head towards it and wander lonely as a cloud to your heart's content, there is no more inviting place in the Southern Highlands.

Paths and terrain are excellent, escape routes are numerous and inter-Munro bealachs are high. All four Munros can be ticked off in a single expedition for barely more upward effort than an ascent of Ben Nevis.

For a less strenuous outing, Meall nan Aighean is the easiest Munro to reach. Once up, Carn Mairg, the next Munro along, is a tempting bonus and from there you can continue as far as your legs will carry you along this great rollercoaster in the sky.

Meall nan Aighean from Invervar
NN 666483, 5ml/8km, 800m/2600ft

Begin at Invervar, 8ml/13km from Coshieville at the foot of Glen Lyon. There's a hidden car park a short distance down a side road just before the telephone box. From here, cross the glen road, go through the iron gate opposite and follow a Land Rover track up through woods on the right-hand (east) side of the Invervar Burn. Leave the track at the first telegraph pole beyond the woods for an excellent path that climbs Meall nan Aighean's south-west ridge, rimming the well-named bowl of Coire a' Chearcaill (*Corra Cyarcle*, Circular Corrie).

At a levelling at a height of 530m/ 1740ft, the path crosses a wider stalkers' path that comes up from the right, crosses the ridge and heads left to a dilapidated hut in the bowl of the corrie. The stalkers' path begins on the approach track 20 metres before the telegraph pole and makes an equally excellent alternative ascent route but, as it stays below the crest of the ridge, we prefer the ridge path for the views.

The curious, beehive-shaped building passed near the start of the walk is a restored eighteenth century lint mill, used to mechanise the production of linen from local flax. Worth a peek.

The path climbs the broadening ridge without incident almost all the

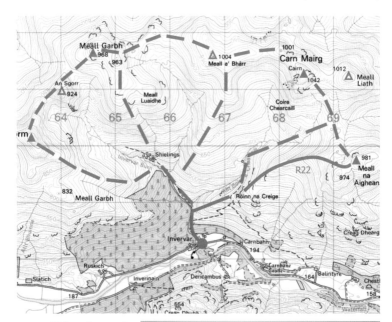

way to Aighean's summit and makes for a pleasant, well-graded ascent. It becomes indistinct higher up but, thanks to short grass underfoot, it is hardly needed. The rocky ▲summit is the further away of two rounded tops, being 7m/23ft higher than its twin.

The path zigzags up Meall nan Aighean's SW Ridge

Chesthill Estate, on whose land the Glen Lyon Horseshoe stands, has a history of restrictive practices towards walkers. The huge iron gate at the start of the walk was padlocked until the Land Reform (Scotland) Act 2003 enforced free access.

The estate now wishes you to walk the horseshoe in a clockwise direction and stay out of all corries and glens! You are not obliged to heed such advice, but do take note of stalking restrictions (mid Aug to 20 Oct, excluding Sundays). Further information is available on local notices or at www.chesthill.com (tel: 01887-830312).

Bonus Munro: Carn Mairg… et al add-on 2ml/3km, 190m/600ft

Viewed from Meall nan Aighean, Carn Mairg, the reigning peak of the Glen Lyon Horseshoe, appears as the leftmost of two rounded rises to the north. It is connected to Meall nan Aighean by a broad, hummocky, 850m/2800ft saddle and is easily reached. The ▲summit is skirted by an awkward boulderfield but, once across the saddle, the path cuts left below the skyline to ascend a grassy rake and find a congenial way up.

For the easiest way back, return to the saddle, descend into Coire Chearcaill and follow the stream down to the hut noted above (marked on OS map at NN 673497). Here you'll pick up the stalkers' path that crosses to Aighean's south-west ridge to rejoin the approach route.

Meall a' Bharr

CARN MAIRG

MEALL NAN AIGHEAN

saddle

Coire a' Chearcaill

Viewed from Meall nan Aighean SW Ridge

To stay higher longer, follow the skyline west to Meall a' Bharr and descend the latter's easy south-west ridge to reach the Invervar Burn.

The end of the Glen Lyon Horseshoe viewed from its start

CARN GORM

Meall nan Aighean SW Ridge

Or, if you're suffering from a surfeit of energy, continue around the Horseshoe to ▲Meall Garbh (*Myowl Garrav*, Rough Hill) and ▲Carn Gorm (*Carn Gorram*, Blue Cairn). A path curves down the latter's south-east ridge to again reach the Invervar Burn (total 11ml/17km, 1450m/ 4750ft).

▲Meall Buidhe 248 932m/3058ft (OS 51, NN 498499)
Myowl Boo-ya, Yellow Hill

Viewed from Stuchd an Lochain N Ridge

If the rounded summits of the Glen Lyon Horseshoe lack the soaring pointiness that some demand in their mountains, the similar but lower summits to their west, punctuating little-visited country on the north side of the upper glen, are even more unremarkable. Only Meall Buidhe heaves itself over the magic 3000ft mark to attract humankind to its lonely top.

Yet we like Meall Buidhe. While some mountains flatter to deceive, unassuming Meall Buidhe scorns vulgar ostentation... which only makes its amazing summit even more remarkable. We're talking about one of the finest viewpoints in the whole Scottish Highlands.

The summit can be reached by a long approach hike from Loch Rannoch to the north, but the most effortless ascent route begins near the head of Glen Lyon to the south. A side road climbs to scenic Loch an Daimh (*Loch an Daff*, Stag Loch), at which point, at a height of 410m/1350ft, you're half-way up the mountain already.

In winter Meall Buidhe's gentle demeanour and high starting point combine to give an easy ascent to a spectacular viewpoint out of all proportion to the effort involved in reaching it. This is an excellent winter route for beginners (adorned with ice axe and crampons glinting in the sunlight, of course).

Meall Buidhe from Loch an Daimh
NN 512464, 5½ml/9km, 520m/1700ft

The route begins just before the end of the side road to Loch an Daimh, where a Land Rover track on the right climbs the hillside in the direction of Meall Buidhe's summit. Follow the track to a T-junction a short distance up, then go left to find the start of a continuing path.

One path (Path 1), hidden among the heather barely ten metres from the T-junction, climbs straight up the hillside to the level skyline above. Leave that for descent and take a second path (Path 2) that begins a few hundred metres further along, at the top of the next rise.

As it climbs the boggy hillside, Path 2 improves and deteriorates in turns. Not until approaching the skyline, which is revealed to be nothing more than the lower ten metres of peaty Coire Beithe (*Corra Bay-a*, Birch Corrie), does it veer left at a gentler angle and reach firmer ground on the corrie's west-bounding ridge.

On the way to the ridge you'll join Path 1, and on the crest of the ridge you'll join yet another path. Note both of these junctions for the return trip. The number of paths that exist on the mountain are testament to decades of attempts to find the best ground.

As height is gained, the ridge splays out across delightful (not!) peat hags, where the path becomes difficult to follow. The most appealing aspect of this part of the route is its brevity.

Even if you lose the path, it soon becomes obvious again on easy grass slopes that rise from the peat to the next skyline. Here you find yourself on the rim of Glas Choire (*Glass Chorra*, Green Corrie), a vast, wide-open north-east corrie that has been hidden from view until now.

Along the rim to the right is rounded Meall a' Phuill (*Myowl a Foo-il*), while to the left is Meall Buidhe's south-east top, an insignificant swelling that was once a former Top in the Tables.

Loch an Daimh was formerly called Loch Giorra. Following its damming for hydro-electric power in the 1950s, its waters backed up to join Loch an Diamh, which was then a smaller loch further up the glen. The dam is called Giorra Dam in memory of the lower loch. Pipelines carry water from Loch an Daimh *under* Stuchd an Lochain to Cashlie in upper Glen Lyon.

The view west from the path up Meall Buidhe

Loch an Daimh

Meall a' Phuill means either
Hill of the Hole (referring
to the depths of Glas
Choire) or Hill of Mud (no
prizes for guessing the
origin of that derivation).

SE top

The path goes left,
well away from the corrie
rim, to make the short
climb to the south-east
top. All that remains then
is a languid stroll around
the continuing rim to its
highest point.

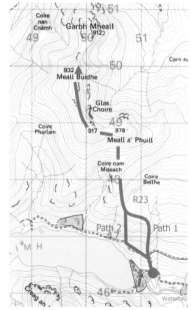

With a glorious view across Rannoch
Moor in front of you, and a new spring
in your step, this final ½ml/1km
saunter across the turf to Meall
Buidhe's ▲summit is not nearly long
enough. You may well spend more
time at the summit, testing your
mountain-spotting prowess, than you
will skipping back down to the road.

On the return trip, you may prefer
to follow the corrie rim all the way
round to the green-baize top of Meall
a' Phuill before descending. If you lose
the path back down among the peat
hags, you'll discover, if you haven't
already on the way up, that just about
every bit of dry ground carries a little
path. Aim for Coire Beithe's west-
bounding ridge and you'll regain the
main path at some point.

After leaving the ridge lower down,
keep left at the junction of Path 1 and
Path 2 to make a round trip. If you
can't find Path 1, or if you lose it, aim

You'll have noted that the road-end
information board of Lochs Estate suggests
using Path 2 only but, in the generally
boggy terrain hereabouts, Path 1 gives a
dry and agreeable descent, so we suggest
that outside the stalking season you make
a round of it (as described) by going up
Path 2 and down Path 1.

The Stress-free Saunter to the Scenic Summit

MEALL BUIDHE

Glas Choire

SE top

for a reedy lochan on the flat ground at the lower rim of Coire Beithe. The path passes its left side and soon

reaches gentle, dry ground that gives an effortless final descent above the shores of Loch an Daimh.

CENTRAL HIGHLANDS

MAMORES   BEN NEVIS   GREY CORRIES

Rannoch Moor

The view north

Meall Buidhe's summit is completely encircled by a virtual roll-call of Southern Highland and Central Highland peaks. Morning is the best time for the incomparable view across The Great

Flatness (Rannoch Moor) to Glen Coe and the Nevis Range. For the full show, make the short return trip across the dip to the north to the nearby rise of Garbh Mheall (*Garrav Vyowl*, Rough Hill).

▲Stuchd an Lochain 197 960m/3150ft (OS 51, NN 483448)
Stoochk an Lochin, Peak of the Lochan

STUCHD
AN LOCHAIN

N Ridge

Loch an Daimh

S tuchd an Lochain stands isolated on the south shore of Loch an Daimh, directly across the water from Meall Buidhe. Hidden from the dam around a corner of the loch, the Stuchd's northern flank rises in one great sweep from the shore, so gouged by glaciation that little of it remains except an enormous craggy corrie (Coire an Lochain, *Corra an Lochin*, Corrie of the Lochan). The

summit perches on the corrie rim, high above a circular lochan and at the apex of a rousing north ridge.

The normal ascent route climbs from the dam to the corrie rim but the path has deteriorated over the years and is now very steep and infuriatingly boggy. The easiest ascent route now lies on the other side of the mountain, where less steep grass slopes climb from Glen Lyon to the corrie rim.

Stuchd an Lochain has a unique claim to fame in that it was the scene of the first ever recorded ascent of a Munro, around 1590. The Munro bagger, more (in)famous for abducting ladies and executing

Macdonalds than for his hillwalking exploits, was Colin 'The Mad' Campbell of Glen Lyon. Although some say you have to be mad to climb mountains, Colin's excuse was to stalk game.

Stuchd an Lochain from Cashlie (Glen Lyon)
NN 490418, 5ml/8km, 660m/2150ft

Park at the east entrance to Cashlie house, at a height of 300m/1000ft in upper Glen Lyon, and walk up the drive. Just before the house, a gate on the right gives access to open hillside on the right-hand side of the Allt Cashlie. Follow this stream all the way up and you'll reach the rim of Coire an Lochain near the summit of the mountain.

STUCHD AN LOCHAIN

An Grianan

Cashlie

Glen Lyon

Viewed from MEALL GHAORDAIDH

The first part of the ascent is steep and pathless but the going is good, on short grass beside a fence. Height is gained fast. Soon you pass the rocky bluffs of An Grianan (*An Gree-anan*, The Sunny Spot), the bold lump of a hill on the left, and enter the wide open spaces of Stuchd an Lochain's broad southern corrie. In contrast to the northern Coire an Lochain, this is so shallow, grassy and featureless that it is easy to lose your bearings in it, even on a clear day.

The going deteriorates somewhat in the bowl of the corrie, but the ground is nowhere near as boggy as might be expected and much drier than on the Loch an Daimh approach. Follow the line of the main stream up and out of the corrie and you'll reach the skyline at the rim of Coire an Lochain, which drops away on the far side of the mountain for a sudden and startling change of scenery.

STUCHD AN LOCHAIN

If you're not sure which is the main stream, just keep heading up the gentle grass slopes and you'll reach the skyline at some point. At the rim of Coire an Lochain the rise to the right is ΔSron Chona Chorein (*Strawn Chonna Chorrin*, Nose of the Meeting of the Corries), while Stuchd an Lochain's summit is to your left (hopefully!).

Now you join the Loch an Daimh approach for the last few hundred metres of the ascent along the corrie rim. The craggy recesses of the inner corrie nestle Lochan nan Cat, which unlike its namesake on Ben Lawers forms an almost perfect circle and doesn't look at all like its eponymous beastie. Beyond a shallow saddle, steeper slopes rise to the Stuchd's distinctive half-dome ▲summit.

Approaching the summit   Sron Chona Chorein

Coire an Lochain

STUCHD
AN LOCHAIN

Alternative Descent add-on 2ml/3km road walk

An Grianan separates Stuchd an Lochain's southern corrie from another shallow corrie (the south-west corrie), down which the Allt Camaslaidh flows to Pubil House, 2ml/3km west of Cashlie on the Glen Lyon road. Pubil is at the same height as Cashlie and is the same distance from the summit of Stuchd an Lochain.

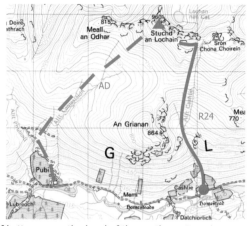

You could climb the mountain from here, but we prefer the ascent from Cashlie on account of better going and better views on the rim of Coire an Lochain. However, providing you don't mind an end-of-day road walk back to Cashlie, a descent to Pubil allows a circuit to be made.

From the summit, descend south-west down easy grass slopes to reach the bowl of the south-west corrie. A smattering of peat bogs has to be negotiated, but aim for the Allt Camaslaidh and you should find reasonable going along its banks. In places a streamside sheep path even encourages speedy progress over gentle terrain.

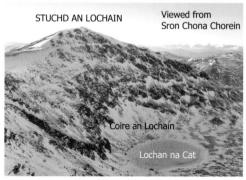

STUCHD AN LOCHAIN   Viewed from
                          Sron Chona Chorein

+ Coire an Lochain

Lochan na Cat

The hillside steepens above the road but the going remains good. At a height of 500m/1650ft you'll come across a hydro road that makes light work of the final 200m/650ft descent to Pubil. The initial long hairpin can be shortcut. Once down, all that remains is the 2ml/3km road walk back to Cashlie.

During the stalking season Lochs Estate wishes you to avoid the route described here and climb Stuchd an Lochain via the standard route from Loch an Daimh.

▲**Schiehallion** 59 1083m/3553ft (OS 42, 51 or 52, NN 714547)
Shee<u>hallion</u>, fancifully translated since Victorian times as Fairy Hill of the Caledonians, from the Gaelic *Sithean* (Pointed Hill or Fairy Hill) and *Chaillean*. With less prudishness and greater fidelity to the mountain's shape, earlier eighteenth century mapmakers translated it as Maiden's Pap, from the Gaelic *Sine* (Breast) and *Chailinn* (Maiden).

We admit it, we don't know what to make of Schiehallion. It certainly dominates its landscape, showing up as a graceful cone from the west and an equally attractive wedge from the Queen's View along Loch Tummel to the east.

It also has a greater historical importance than most. Even the Ordnance Survey succumbs to the mountain's exalted opinion of itself and features it, uniquely, on *three* separate maps.

Yet when you climb the thing, it turns out to be nothing more than a great muckle lump, with a long whale-back ridge of irritating broken quartzite that rises over an irritating succession of irritating false summits. Did we mention it was irritating? But then again, there's that nice new approach path, and that extensive summit view over loch and woodland, unhampered by surrounding mountains...

Maybe you'd better just go see for yourself. If ever a mountain needed to be climbed *because it is there*, it is Schiehallion.

Schiehallion from Braes of Foss
NN 753557, 6ml/10km, 760m/2500ft

From Schiehallion's conical summit, the whaleback east ridge tilts down to a shoulder, below which the ascent route begins at a car park near Braes of Foss farm, at a height of 330m/1080ft (small parking fee payable at machine). No route in the Scottish Highlands has two such contrasting halves, with a brilliant new path up to the shoulder and execrable going beyond.

The path was built by the John Muir Trust at a cost of £817,000, following the purchase of the north-east side of the mountain in 1999. With its surface of compacted gravel, it is a vast improvement on the boggy morass of the old path and a joy to walk.

SCHIEHALLION

E Ridge

NW Ridge

In the eighteenth century the Astronomer Royal Nevil Maskelyne made use of Schiehallion's regular shape to seek evidence in support of Newton's gravitational theories. A previous such experiment on the Ecuadoran volcano Chimborazo in 1749 had proved too difficult to manage, but Schiehallion magnanimously rose to the challenge.

Maskelyne spent four months on the mountain in 1774, taking a number of astronomical observations at various locations to see how much they were affected by gravitational pull. From these readings he was able to estimate Schiehallion's mass and extrapolate from that to the mass of the earth and other bodies in the solar system.

In support of the experiment, Charles Hutton was given the task of surveying the mountain. To simplify presentation of his findings he came up with the idea of joining points of equal height on the map, and in so doing he invented contour lines.

The new path from
Braes of Foss

The path crosses the moor and wends its way up the shoulder for around 2ml/3½km (3400m to be precise). It ends at a height of 830m/2720ft, at a junction with the old path and the start of the

whaleback ridge. A short distance beyond here, at NN 726545, the horseshoe-shaped memorial known as the Maskelyne Cairn commemorates one of the Astronomer Royal's observation points.

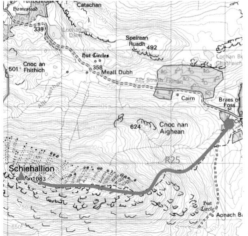

The character of the route changes completely when you set foot on the quartzite and begin the prolonged plod up the rockpile of the east ridge, from false summit to false summit. The slope is gentle but the terrain is anything but. A stony line worn among the rocks by generations of hillwalkers attempts to find the least aggravating going but, when the rocks become too jumbled, especially higher up, you'll be left to your own devices.

As distraction, the view behind opens up over a great tranche of lowland to the Cairngorms. And you can always spur yourself on with some creative visualisation of the even more expansive view that awaits at the summit.

The classic view from the west

SCHIEHALLION

E Ridge

NW Ridge

Loch Rannoch

The ▲summit cairn itself is perched atop a short ridge of tilted quartzite pavement that drops in tiers of small crags to the south. Take care when exploring, especially if the slippery rock is wet.

Looking back down the E Ridge

Braes of Foss
←

SCHIEHALLION
Summit

Memo to self: Request JMT to extend the new path all the way to the summit.

After pausing at the summit to take in the view westwards, which is as wide-ranging as you would expect from a pyramid summit on the edge of Rannoch Moor, and to debate the mountain's worth, all you have to do then is descend. Some find the rubble more infuriating to negotiate on the way down than on the way up, which gives Schiehallion another claim to fame. It is a mountain on which, uniquely, you may well find yourself asking someone coming up: 'Is it far to the bottom?'

Somewhere on
SCHIEHALLION

At NN 752553, beside the path on the right, c.200m from the gate at the end of the car park, an isolated cup-marked boulder lies among the bracken. It is thought that the many small hollows or 'cups' were carved into the rock pre-Bronze Age, between 3000BC and 2000BC, but their purpose remains a mystery. Art, cartography, ritual... you decide.

The sheep fanks further along, at the foot of the path's first steepening (NN 748547), date from the beginning of the nineteenth century, when sheep began to replace cattle as the mainstay of Highland life. Several hundred metres south of here at NN 747540, off-route along an old Land Rover track, is the hut circle of Aonach Ban (*Ernach Bahn*, White Ridge), dating from c.1500BC to early AD. Other archaeological findings dot Schiehallion's mountainsides. For further information, visit www.jmt.org/east-schiehallion-estate.asp.

INDEX

Luath Press Limited
committed to publishing well written books worth reading

LUATH PRESS takes its name from Robert Burns, whose little collie Luath (*Ga*
swift or nimble) tripped up Jean Armour at a wedding and gave him the chance
speak to the woman who was to be his wife and the abiding love of his
life. Burns called one of 'The Twa Dogs' Luath after Cuchullin's
hunting dog in Ossian's *Fingal*. Luath Press was established
in 1981 in the heart of Burns country, and now resides
a few steps up the road from Burns' first lodgings on
Edinburgh's Royal Mile.
Luath offers you distinctive writing with a hint of unexpected pleasures.

Most bookshops in the UK, the US, Canada, Australia,
New Zealand and parts of Europe either carry our
books in stock or can order them for you. To order direct from
us, please send a £sterling cheque, postal order, international
money order or your credit card details (number, address of
cardholder and expiry date) to us at the address below. Please add
post and packing as follows: UK – £1.00 per delivery address;
overseas surface mail – £2.50 per delivery address; overseas
airmail – £3.50 for the first book to each delivery address, plus £1.00 for each
additional book by airmail to the same address. If your order is a gift, we will happ
enclose your card or message at no extra charge.

Luath Press Limited
543/2 Castlehill
The Royal Mile
Edinburgh EH1 2ND
Scotland
Telephone: 0131 225 4326 (24 hours)
Fax: 0131 225 4324
email: sales@luath.co.uk
Website: www.luath.co.uk